The First World War in Africa 1914-1918

The First World War in Africa 1914-1918

Togoland, South-West Africa, the Cameroons
& East Africa

ILLUSTRATED WITH PICTURES & MAPS

John Buchan

LEONAUR

The First World War in Africa 1914-1918
Togoland, South-West Africa, the Cameroons & East Africa
by John Buchan

ILLUSTRATED WITH PICTURES & MAPS

FIRST EDITION

Leonaur is an imprint of Oakpast Ltd

Copyright in this form © 2018 Oakpast Ltd

ISBN: 978-1-78282-708-5 (hardcover)
ISBN: 978-1-78282-709-2 (softcover)

http://www.leonaur.com

Publisher's Notes

Contents

CHAPTER 1

German Aims in Africa

By the end of August, 1914, the war had spread beyond Europe to every quarter of the globe where Germany possessed a square mile of territory. British Australasian and African dominions were engaged in defending or enlarging their borders, and, though the fighting was on a small scale compared with the gigantic European struggle, it had important strategical bearings, and for Britain was scarcely less vital than the battlefields of France. We propose to consider the campaigns conducted in the different parts of Africa, where Germany owned four colonies, contiguous to those of France and Britain. This was fighting of a familiar type, such as almost every year had shown on some portion of the Empire's frontiers. The British fought with and against armies largely composed of native troops and the country was that bush and desert which had been for a century the common theatre of our armed adventures.

Germany's colonial ambitions awoke with her great development after the victory over France in the Franco-Prussian War. She desired to emulate Britain in finding an outlet under her flag for her surplus population, which had hitherto emigrated to North and South America; she wished to have producing grounds of her own from which she could draw raw material for her new factories; she sought to share in the glory of conquest and colonization, which had done so much for France and Britain; and, as a coming maritime power, she was anxious to have something for her navy to defend. Her thinkers as well as her statesmen fostered the new interest. List and Friedel and Treitschke pointed out that trade followed the flag, and that the flag might also follow trade; while Bismarck discerned in the movement a chance of getting fresh assets to bargain with in that European game which he played with such consummate skill. Especially Germany's eyes turned towards Africa, and not without justification. Her travellers had been among the greatest pioneers of that mysterious continent.

In the history of South African exploration honourable place must be given to the names of Kolbe and Lichtenstein, Mohr and Mauch. In West and Northern Africa, the roll of honour contained such great adventurers as Hornemann and Barth, Ziegler and Schweinfurth, Rohlfs and Nachtigal. It was a German, Karl von der Decken, who first surveyed Kilimanjaro, and the story of African enterprise contains few more heroic figures than that of von Wissmann. Germany was resolved to share in what is called the scramble for Africa, and she had admirable pathfinders in her missionaries and explorers.

This is not the place to describe in detail the tortuous events from 1880 onwards which led to the foundation of the four German African colonies. It is a fascinating tale, for Germany made adroit use of the suspicions and supineness of the Powers in possession. So far as the British Governments of the day were concerned, she might have had all she wanted for the asking; and it was only by the efforts of clear-sighted private citizens that her bolder schemes were checkmated. Her first attempts were directed towards the Portuguese colony of Delagoa Bay, which would bring her in touch with what she believed to be the bitterly anti-British people of the Transvaal.

In Pondoland and at St. Lucia Bay, on the Zululand coast, she endeavoured to get grants of land from the native chiefs, and was only stopped by a tardy British intervention, forced upon the mother-country by the people of Cape Colony. Few at home realised the significance of the attempts, and Mr. Gladstone in the House of Commons publicly thanked God for them, and looked forward to her alliance, "in the execution of the great purposes of Providence for the advantage of mankind."

In 1884 the work was fairly begun. Sir Bartle Frere from Cape Town had warned Lord Carnarvon as early as 1878 that Britain must be mistress up to the Portuguese frontier on both the east and west coasts. He wrote:

> There is no escaping from the responsibility which has been already incurred ever since the English flag was planted on the castle here. All our difficulties have arisen, and still arise, from attempting to evade or shift this responsibility.

But presently Herr Luderitz had founded his settlement at Luderitz Bay, and on April 25, 1884, the German flag was hoisted in

Damaraland, and the colony of German South-West Africa was constituted. Two months later Nachtigal landed from a gunboat at Lome, the port of Togoland, and by arrangement with the local chiefs declared the country a German Protectorate. A month after he did the same thing in the Cameroons, and the British consul, sent to frustrate him, arrived five days too late.

Bismarck, desiring to regularise his acquisitions, summoned the famous Berlin Conference, which met on 15th November of the same year. Many of its phrases are still in common use—"Occupation to be valid must be effective," "Spheres of influence," and such like. Meanwhile German agents, including the notorious Karl Peters, were busy in Zanzibar, intriguing with the *Sultan*, and sending expeditions into the interior to secure concessions. Someday the history will be written of the part played in that contest by men like Sir Frederick Lugard, who, while they could not prevent the creation of German East Africa, saved Uganda and the East African Protectorate for Britain.

In 1890 came the Caprivi Agreement, as a consequence of which Heligoland was ceded to Germany. It settled the boundaries of German East Africa, but it did more, for it gave to German South-West Africa a strip of land running north-east to the Zambesi, which formed a wedge separating the Bechuanaland Protectorate from Angola and North-West Rhodesia.

There could be no objection in international law or ethics to Germany's African activity, though there might be much to her methods of conducting it. She had a right to get as much territory as she could, and to profit by the blindness of her rivals. But by 1890 a new and more watchful spirit was appearing in British Africa, and to some extent in the mother-country. Cecil Rhodes was beginning his great struggle with Paul Kruger for the road to the north, and the dream of a Cape to Cairo route seized upon the popular imagination. Imperialists sighed for a Monroe doctrine for Africa, but the day for that had long gone by.

A solid German fence had been built across that northern avenue which might have joined up Nyassaland and North-East Rhodesia with Uganda and the Sudan. Meanwhile Germany, having got her colonies, did not handle them with great discretion. She was much out of pocket over them, for she lavished money on the construction of roads and railways, and especially on that cast-iron type of administration which was the Prussian ideal. Her first blunder was her treatment of her settlers, who found themselves terribly swathed in red tape, and were apt to trek over the border to more liberal British climes. Her second was her attitude towards the native population.

Unaccustomed to allow ancient modes of life to continue side by side with the new—which is the British plan—she attempted to make of the Bantu peoples decorous citizens on the Prussian model; and, when they objected, gave them a taste of Prussian rigour. One of the ablest of German students of colonial policy, Dr. Moritz Bonn of Munich, has noted the result so far as concerns South-West Africa:

> We solved the native problem by smashing tribal life and by creating a scarcity of labour.

Beginning from the west, the first colony, Togoland, is about the size of Ireland, and is bounded on one side by French Dahomey, and on the other by the British Gold Coast. It is shaped like a pyramid, with its narrow end on the sea, for its coast line is only thirty-two miles. About a million natives inhabit it, chiefly Hausas, and the whites number about four hundred. It was a thriving little colony, with a docile and industrious population, and a large trade in palm oil, cocoa, rubber, and cotton, while the natives were considerable owners of cattle, sheep, and goats.

One railway ran inland from Lome, and there was a network of admirable roads, which were a credit to any tropical country. Farther south the German Cameroons lay between British Nigeria and French Congo, and extended from Lake Chad in the north to the Ubangi and Congo rivers. Its area was about one-third larger than the German Empire in Europe, and its population of 3,500,000 contained 2,000 whites, and the rest Bantu and Sudanese tribes. In the south lay the Spanish enclave of Rio Muni, or Spanish Guinea, which was an enclave owing to the arrangements which followed the trouble with France over Morocco in 1911, when Germany obtained a long, narrow strip of French Congo to the south and east of the Cameroons.

This Naboth's vineyard was one of the pieces of territory which Bernhardi had marked down for speedy German acquisition. The Cameroons was a colony of great possibilities, for it contains a range of high mountains, which might form a health station for white residents, while the soil is rich and water abundant. Its products were much the same as Togoland, but its forests provided also valuable timber, and there was a certain mineral development. Some roads had been made, and 150 miles of railway, but trouble with the native tribes had done much to handicap progress.

Following the western coastline past the Congo mouth and the Portuguese territory of Angola, we reach a more important colony in German South-West Africa. Its area is some 320,000 square miles, considerably larger than the Cameroons, and it stretches from the Angola border to its march with Cape Colony on the Orange River. Its native population used to be 300,000, but at the beginning of the war, owing to the Herero campaign, it was little over 100,000—chiefly Bushmen, Hottentots, and Ovambo; while the whites numbered 15,000 and included many agricultural settlers. German South-West Africa was the only German colony where the small farmer, as opposed to the planter, seemed to flourish. In spite of the dryness of the climate the land makes excellent pasturage, and there is considerable mineral wealth in the shape of copper and diamonds.

The latter were discovered in 1906 near Luderitz Bay, and promised at one time to become a serious competitor to the mines of Kimberley and the Transvaal. The colony has two chief ports—Swakopmund, halfway down the coast-line, and just north of the little British enclave of Walfish Bay, and Luderitz Bay, or Angra Pequena, nearer the southern border. The capital, Windhoek, is 200 miles from the coast, in a direct line east from Swakopmund.

Some note must be taken of the railways, which were built with a strategical as well as a commercial purpose. A railway quadrilateral had been formed, of which the northern side was Swakopmund to Windhoek, the eastern Windhoek to Keetmanshoop, and the southern Keetmanshoop to Luderitz Bay. From Swakopmund an unfinished line runs for several hundred miles northeast towards the Caprivi strip which abuts on the Zambesi. But the most important strategical extension is in the south, where a branch runs from Reitfontein to Warmbad, which is within easy distance of the Orange River and the frontier of the Cape Province.

The last and greatest of the German colonies is German East Africa, which is about twice the size of European Germany. It has a population of 8,000,000, which includes in normal times about 5,000 white men. The wide variations of climate and landscape which it contains give it endless possibilities. Its northern frontier runs from the coast south of Mombasa, just north of the great snow mass of Kilimanjaro, to the Victoria Nyanza, of which two-thirds are in German territory. Going westward, it includes the eastern shores of Lakes Kivu and Tanganyika, as well as the north-eastern shore of Lake Nyassa. It has Britain for its neighbour on the north and part of the west borders,

GOLD COAST REGIMENT

while the remainder of the west marches with the Belgian Congo and the whole of the south with Portuguese Mozambique.

The islands of Pemba and Zanzibar, under British protection, dominate the northern part of its coastline of 620 miles. It will be seen that the vast lake region of the west provides admirable means of transit, and is eminently suitable for tropical agriculture. Elsewhere water is a difficulty, for the only river of any size is the Rufiji, and the snows of Kilimanjaro largely drain towards British territory. Nevertheless, it is a land of great potential agricultural and pastoral wealth; its forest riches are enormous; gold is known to exist in large quantities, as well as base metals and soda deposits. On this colony Germany especially, expended money and care. It was resolved to make it a planter's country, and huge agricultural estates were the rule.

Four excellent ports, Lindi, Kilwa, Tanga, and the capital, Dar-es-Salam, made commerce easy, and the colony was well served by the great German steamship lines. Two railways ran into the interior, and competed with the Uganda railway to Port Florence. One, running from Tanga to Moschi, served the rich foothills of Kilimanjaro, and was destined to be continued to Victoria Nyanza. A second, which was only completed in 1914, ran from Dar-es-Salam to Tabora, an important junction of caravan routes, and was continued thence to Ujiji, on Tanganyika. All such railways were intended under happier circumstances to be connected at their railheads by the great Cape to Cairo route. It will be seen that, if in West Africa Germany had acquired no more than ordinary tropical colonies, and in South-West Africa something of a white elephant, in East Africa she had won a territory which might someday be among the richest of African possessions.

The first blow in the war was struck in Togoland. That small colony was in an impossible strategic position, with French and British territory enveloping it on three sides, and a coast-line open to the attack of British warships. Its military forces were at the outside 250 whites and 3,000 natives. In the early days of August, a British cruiser summoned Lome, and the town surrendered without a blow. The German forces fell back one hundred miles inland to Atakpame, where was situated Kamina, one of the chief German overseas wireless stations. Meantime Captain Bryant of the Royal Artillery had led part of the Gold Coast Regiment across the western frontier in motor cars, while the French in Dahomey had entered on the east.

By Monday, the 10th of August, the whole of southern Togoland was in the hands of the Allies, and Captain Bryant, with a small French

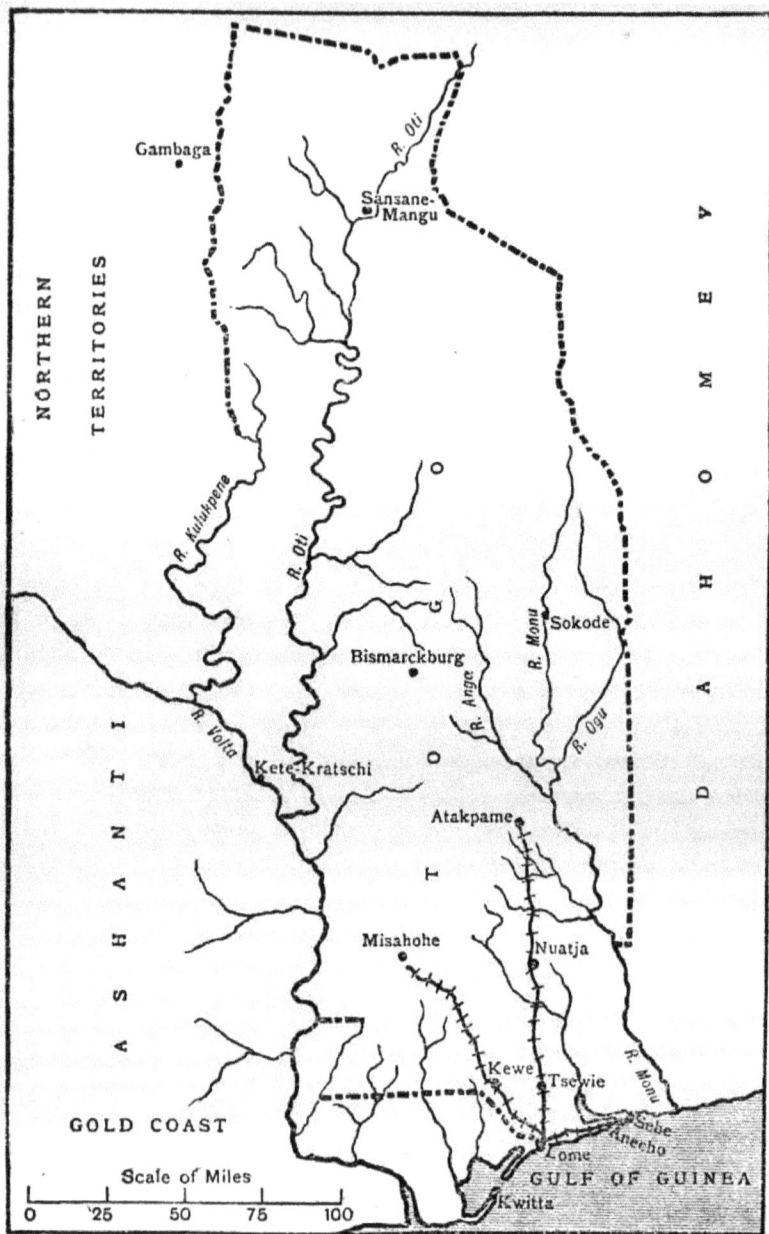

Togoland.

contingent, advanced against the Government station of Atakpame. On 25th August he crossed the River Monu, and by 27th August, with very few casualties, he occupied Atakpame, destroyed the wireless station, and secured the unconditional surrender of the German troops. Togoland had become a colony of the Allies, normal trade was resumed, and in two months' time there was nothing to distinguish it from Dahomey and the Gold Coast.

A far more difficult problem was presented by the Cameroons. Strategically this colony also was hemmed in by the Allies, but the great distances and the difficulty of communication made a concerted scheme not easy to execute. It was arranged that two French columns should move from French Congo, while the British columns should enter at several points on the Nigerian frontier. There is reason to believe that both on the French and British side the advance was made without adequate preparation. It was the rainy season in West Africa, and any campaign in a tangled and ill-mapped country was liable to awkward surprises. A mounted infantry detachment of the West African Frontier Force left Kano on 8th August, under the command of Lieutenant-Colonel Maclear, and seems to have crossed the frontier on 25th August after a heavy march, and occupied the the German post of Tepe, on the Benue River.

Next day it advanced along the Benue as far as Saratse, and on the 29th attacked the river station of Garua. One fort was captured, but next day the Germans counter-attacked in force, and drove back the British troops to Nigerian soil. In this fighting Lieutenant-Colonel Maclear and four other British officers were killed, several were wounded or missing, and forty *per cent*, of the native force was lost. Apparently, we suffered chiefly from Maxim fire, for the Germans, having once located our trenches, had the exact range, and simply mowed down our troops. In the words of one of the survivors:

> It was a terrible loss, and there was absolutely no glory in the whole fighting, taking place as it did in a little out-of-the-way spot 5,000 miles from England, that not one person in a thousand has ever heard of.

No better luck attended the other two expeditions which about the same time entered from Nigeria at more westerly points on the frontier. One entering from Ikom met with little resistance, and about the 30th occupied the German station of Nsanakong, five miles from the border. The other expedition, moving in from Calabar close to the

BRITISH AFRICAN TROOPSS

coast, occupied Archibong on 29th August. A week later, at Nsana-kong, as at Garua, the Germans counter-attacked in force. They arrived about two in the morning, and met with a stubborn resistance until the British ammunition was exhausted, when the garrison endeavoured to cut its way out with the bayonet. The bulk of them managed to retreat to Nigeria, but three British officers and one hundred natives were killed, and many were taken prisoners. Thereupon the Germans crossed the frontier, and occupied the Nigerian station of Okuri, north-east of Calabar, from which, however, they soon retired.

The land attack having failed, recourse was had to the sea. For some time, the British warships *Cumberland* and *Dwarf* had been watching the mouth of the Cameroon River and the approaches to the German port, Duala. On 14th September a bold attempt was made to blow up the *Dwarf* by an infernal machine. Two days later, a German merchantman, the *Nachtigal*, tried to ram the British gunboat, but was wrecked, with the loss of thirty-six men. A few days later two German launches made another attempt with spar-torpedoes, but once again the attack miscarried.

On 27th September the Anglo-French force appeared before Duala, and the bombardment resulted in its unconditional surrender. Bonaberi, the neighbouring coast town, fell to an Anglo-French force, under Brigadier-General Dobell, and the *Cumberland* captured eight merchantmen belonging to the Woermann and Hamburg-Amerika lines. All were in the Cameroon River, and were reported to be in good order, "most of them containing general and homeward cargoes, and considerable quantities of coal."

At the same time a German gunboat, the *Soden*, probably constructed for river work, was seized, and put into commission in the British navy. Meanwhile the French, operating from Libreville in French Congo, and covered by the warship *Surprise*, attacked Ukoko on Corisco Bay, and sank two armed vessels, the *Khios* and the *Itolo*.

With the chief port in our hands, and the coast as a base, the Allies could now advance with better hopes of success. The Germans retreated by the valley of the River Wuri, and by the two interior railways. During October the half-circle of conquered territory was rapidly widened, while isolated entries were made from the northern and southern frontiers. Jabassi, on the Wuri, was taken, and Japoma, the railway terminus. The British had now the measure of the enemy, and could afford to advance at their leisure. By 1st October the Cameroons, so far as it was of any value to Germany in the struggle, was

17

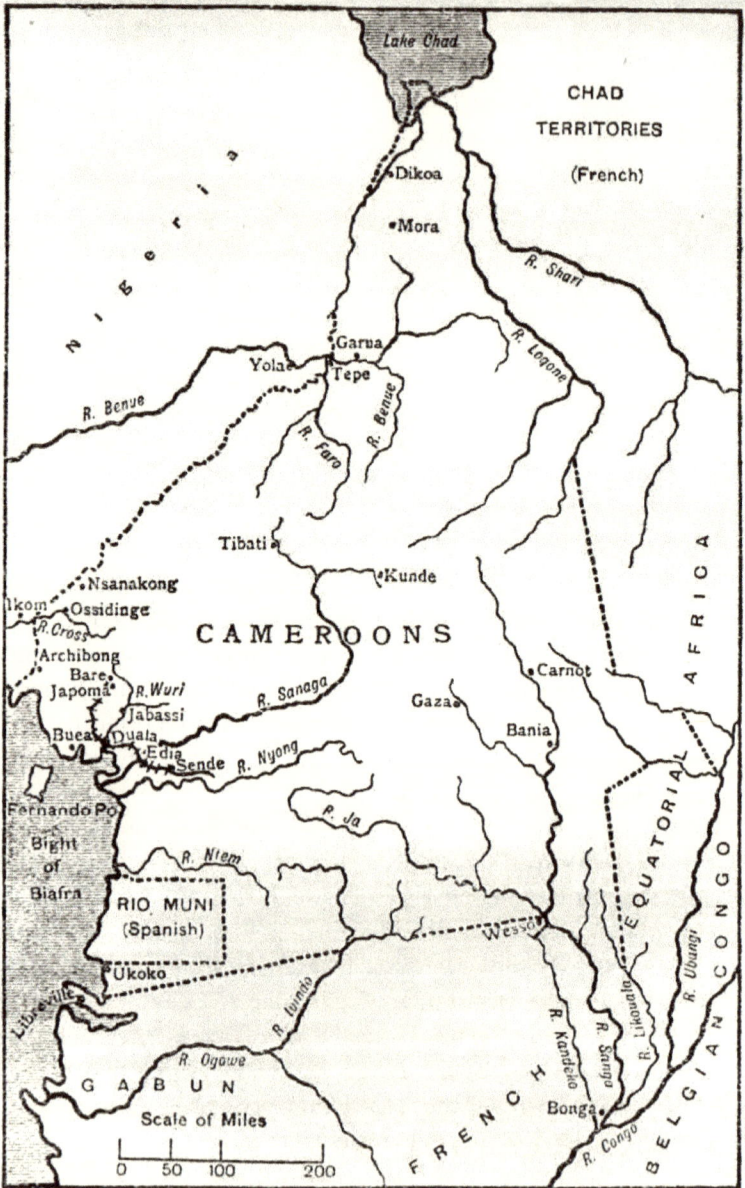

The Cameroons.

virtually captured. The wireless stations had been destroyed, the coast was ours, and the German troops were reduced to defensive warfare in a difficult hinterland.

In German South-West Africa the situation was different from that in the other German colonies of the East and West. Here over the frontier lay not a British Crown possession, but a self-governing dominion. Elsewhere a cable from the Colonial Office could mobilize the British defence, but in South Africa there was an independent Parliament and a hotchpotch of parties to be persuaded. Further, the ground had been carefully baited. Intrigues had been long afoot among the irreconcilable elements in the Dutch population, and the highest of German authorities had not thought it undignified to speak words in season, and to hold out hopes of a new and greater Afrikander republic.

Elsewhere the German colonies had to fight their battles unaided, but here there was every expectation of powerful assistance from within the enemy's camp. Till the situation developed the campaign on Germany's part must be defensive, and for this role German South-West Africa had many advantages. Her capital was far inland, and, since she could hope for no assistance by sea, it mattered little if her ports were seized. Her railways on the south ran down almost to the Cape frontier, but between the Cape railheads and her border stretched the desert of the Kalahari, and the dry and waterless plains of North-West Cape Colony.

At least two hundred miles separated the branch railways at Carnarvon and Prieska from the nearest German territory, and the distance from Kimberley on the main northern line was little less than four hundred. At one point only had the British forces reasonable means of access by land. From Port Nolloth a line runs inland to serve the copper lands of Namaqualand, and from one station on it, Steinkopf, a sixty-mile track leads to Raman's Drift, on the Orange River, a point about fifty miles from the terminus of the German railway at Warmbad.

As to the German forces, it is not possible to speak with certainty. In their official returns before the war they claimed a military force of some 3,500 men, mainly whites; but by calling up reserves and enrolling volunteers from among the civil population of German blood they probably increased this to not less than 6,000. The figure may have been higher, for the Cape Town estimates put the German strength at not less than 10,000, as well as a camel corps 500 strong. The Germans

German Camel Corps

were believed to be strong in artillery, and to have sixty-six batteries of Maxims, half of which were concentrated at Keetmanshoop, in the south of the colony. On the declaration of war, the German governor, Dr. Seitz, put at once into force the long-prepared scheme of defence. The Germans, about 10th August, abandoned their two principal stations on the coast, Swakopmund and Luderitz Bay, and retired with all military stores to their inland capital of Windhoek. Before leaving they destroyed the jetty, and dismantled and sank the tugs in the harbour of Swakopmund. By 20th August they had made small incursions into British territory, entrenching themselves in certain places among the *kopjes*, and skirmishing with the frontier farmers. When General Botha met the Union Parliament on 8th September he was able to inform it that Germany had begun hostilities.

In a later chapter we shall consider the political situation in the Union of South-West Africa which led to a dramatic and not unexpected rebellion. Here it is sufficient to say that General Botha, in a speech of great dignity and force, announced that after careful consideration he and his colleagues had decided to carry the war into German territory, "in the interests of South Africa as well as of the Empire." He had information about German machinations which was denied to the ordinary politician, and the great majority of the members of Parliament were ready to trust his judgment.

The sole opposition came from General Hertzog, who succeeded in mustering only twelve votes in the House of Assembly and five in the Senate. Yet it is clear that his views were largely held in the country, and that many *burghers* looked with alarm upon a policy of active operations. These men lived chiefly in the districts bordering upon German South-West Africa, in the Orange Free State, and in the Western Transvaal, and they argued that, as long as Germany left Union territory alone, no offensive measures should be taken against her. It did not require any great amount of political acumen to foresee that such an attitude was impossible. Sleeping dogs may be best left alone, but when ninety-nine of the pack are tearing in full cry across Europe it is folly to suppose that the hundredth will continue its slumbers.

The beginning of September saw scattered fighting in the southeastern angle of the frontier. Information was received that a considerable German force was advancing to Raman's Drift, on the Orange, with the intention of entrenching themselves and disputing the northward passage of British troops. Colonel Dawson, with the 4th South

SOUTH AFRICAN CAVALRY TRAVELLING OVER SAND-DUNES

African Rifles, left the Port Nolloth railway at Steinkopf, marched the sixty miles to the river, and surprised a German garrison at the drift on 15th September.

After a fight in which only one man was killed, he captured the German blockhouse, and received the surrender of the garrison. He sent patrols up the Orange, and ousted the enemy from the *kopjes*, while with a larger force he compelled the Germans to evacuate an entrenched position farther north. To set against this success, the Germans on 17th September surprised a small British post at Nakob, a point near the Orange just outside the south-eastern angle of the frontier. The victors carried off some cattle and a number of prisoners, and retired, leaving a small garrison. The next day witnessed a British counter-stroke by sea. On 18th September a force sailing to Luderitz Bay occupied the town, and hoisted the Union Jack on the town hall. The Germans had destroyed the wireless station, but otherwise the place was undamaged.

While this frontier fighting was taking place, there was a widespread martial enthusiasm throughout the Union. General Botha, who had agreed to take command of the army, called for 7,000 men— 5,000 foot and 2,000 mounted infantry—and to his appeal there was an immediate and adequate response. Recruiting was stimulated by the news of three unimportant German raids, two across the Orange at Pella and Rietfontein, which they occupied, and one upon Walfish Bay, which failed disastrously. Meantime the Rhodesian Police had occupied the far north-western post of Schuckmansburg, in the Caprivi strip, and had forestalled any danger from that quarter. At this time the strategical idea seems to have been a British advance simultaneously from Rhodesia, down the Orange River and from the Port Nolloth railway, while a movement would also be made inland from the coast ports.

With the end of September there came heavier fighting. On the 27th, between Kolmanskop and Grassplatz, a German patrol was surprised by some Rand Light Infantry, and found its retreat barred by a body of Imperial Light Horse. In the skirmish three British and four Germans were killed. Our forces in this affair were operating from Luderitz Bay, and, using the same base, we surprised a German post at Anichab. Meantime, at the south-eastern angle a more serious encounter took place which ended in a British reverse. Between Warmbad and Raman's Drift lies a place called Sandfontein, important as one of the few spots where water can be got in that arid desert.

German Askari troops

On 25th September a small force of South African Mounted Rifles and Transvaal Horse Artillery pushed forward to the water-hole, which lay in a cup-shaped hollow, commanded by *kopjes*, and with the only retreat through an awkward defile. Early on the 26th the Germans brought up guns to the heights, and till noon bombarded the water-hole, while a considerable force held the pass in the rear. The British troops, under Colonel Grant, made a gallant fight till their ammunition was exhausted, and then, having first rendered their guns useless, were forced to surrender. The British total strength seems to have been no more than 200, and out of it lost 16 killed, 43 wounded, and a large number of prisoners and missing. The German commander, Lieutenant-Colonel von Heydebreck, behaved like a good soldier, complimented the survivors on their defence, and buried the British dead with the honours of war.

The affair at Sandfontein was in many ways mysterious. It looked as if we had had false information, or treacherous guides, to have been betrayed into so hopeless a battle. A fortnight later came news which explained much and revealed a very ugly state of things in the north-west of the Cape Province. The British forces there were under the command of a certain Lieutenant-Colonel S. G. Maritz, who had fought on the Dutch side in the South African War, and had assisted the Germans in their struggles with the Hereros.

Maritz was the ordinary type of soldier of fortune, not uncommon in South Africa, florid, braggart, gallant after his fashion, and with little scientific knowledge of war. General Botha found reason to suspect his loyalty, and dispatched Colonel Conrad Brits to take over his command. Maritz refused to come in, and challenged Colonel Brits to come himself and relieve him. The latter sent Major Ben Bouwer as his deputy, who was made prisoner by Maritz, but subsequently released, and sent back with an ultimatum to the Union Government. This ultimatum declared that, unless the Government guaranteed that before a certain date Generals Hertzog, De Wet, Beyers, Kemp, and Muller should be allowed to come and meet him and give him their instructions, he would forthwith invade the Union.

Major Bouwer had other interesting matters to report. To quote the dispatch of the Governor-General:

Maritz was in possession of some guns belonging to the Germans, and held the rank of general commanding the German troops. He had a force of Germans under him, in addition to

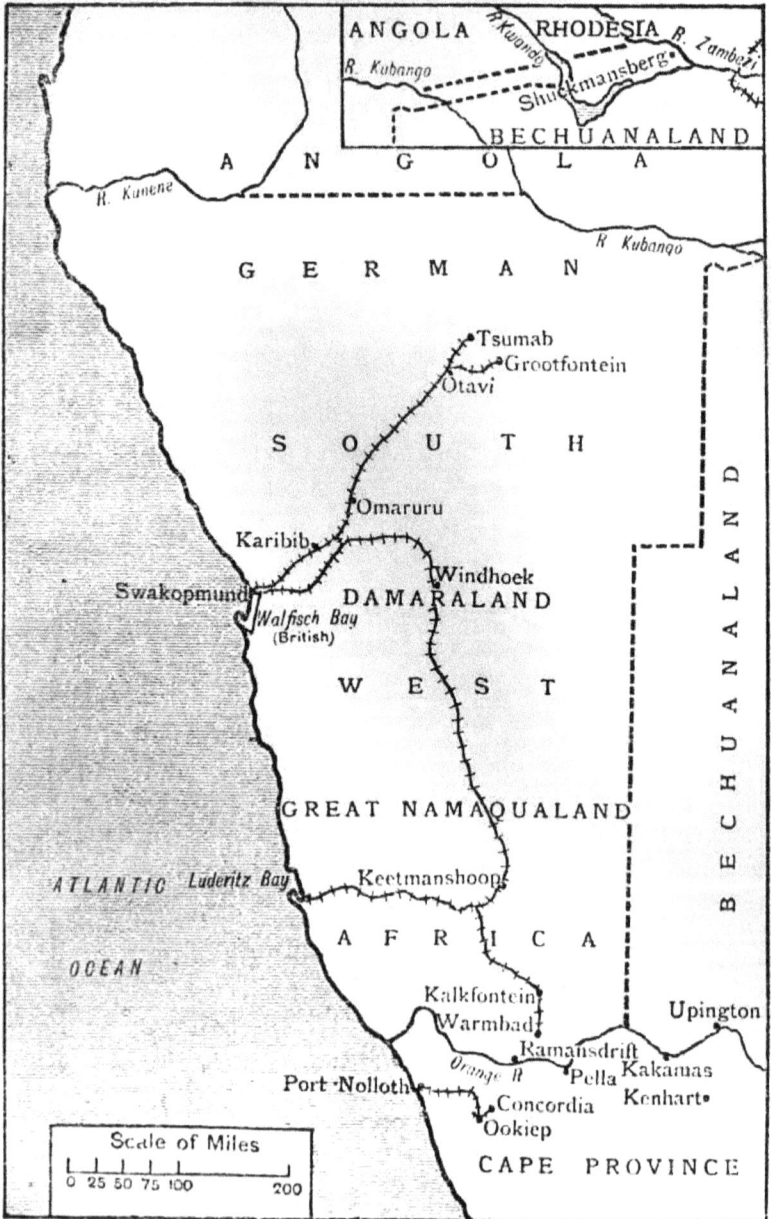

ANGOLA RHODESIA R. Zambezi

R. Kwando

R. Kubango

Shuckmansberg

BECHUANALAND

A N G O L A

R. Kunene

G E R M A N

R. Kubango

Tsumab

Grootfontein

Otavi

S O U T H

Omaruru

Karibib

Windhoek

Swakopmund

DAMARALAND

Walfisch Bay
(British)

W E S T

GREAT NAMAQUALAND

ATLANTIC Luderitz Bay

Keetmanshoop

OCEAN

A F R I C A

Kalkfontein

Warmbad

Upington

Ramansdrift

Orange R. Kakamas

Pella

Port Nolloth

Concordia Kenhart

Ookiep

B E C H U A N A L A N D

Scale of Miles

0 25 50 75 100   200

CAPE PROVINCE

German South West Africa.

his own rebel commando. He had arrested all those of his officers and men who were unwilling to join the Germans, and had then sent them forward as prisoners to German South-West Africa. Major Bouwer saw an agreement between Maritz and the Governor of German South-West Africa, guaranteeing the independence of the Union as a republic, ceding Walfish Bay and certain other portions of the Union to the Germans, and undertaking that the Germans would only invade the Union on the invitation of Maritz. Major Bouwer was shown numerous telegrams and helio messages dating back to the beginning of September. Maritz boasted that he had ample guns, rifles, ammunition, and money from the Germans, and that he would overrun the whole of South Africa.

The immediate result of this discovery was the proclamation of martial law throughout the Union and a general strengthening of the Union forces. The time had now come for every man in South Africa to reveal where lay his true sympathies, and the centre of action was soon to shift from the western borders to the very theatre where for three years the British Army had striven against the present generalissimo of the Union forces. Meantime Maritz proved a broken reed to his new allies. His one asset was an intimate local knowledge of the waterless north-west. He had small notion of serious warfare, and was incompetent to control his ill-assorted forces. He fixed his base near Upington, on the Orange, and dispatched a portion of his command of 2,000 to march southward up the Great Fish River against Kenhart and Calvinia.

Colonel Brits lost no time in harrying the Upington commando, and on 15th October captured a part of it at Ratedrai, many of the men voluntarily surrendering. On the 22nd Maritz attacked Keimoes, a British station on the Orange, south-west of Upington. But its small garrison of 150, after holding on till reinforcements reached it, drove him back, and captured four of his officers. Maritz then moved west down the Orange to Kakamas, where Colonel Brits fell upon him so fiercely that he lost all his tents and stores, and was compelled to withdraw, wounded, over the German frontier.

He made another sally on the 30th, but was conclusively beaten by Brits at Schuit Drift, and driven finally out of the colony. Meantime the commando which had marched up the Great Fish River had no better success. It travelled fast, and by 25th October had covered 200

King's African Rifles

miles, and was close to Calvinia. Here Colonel van der Venter beat it heavily, taking ninety prisoners and the two Maxim guns, which Maritz had confiscated from the Union Army. The commando was hopelessly broken, and "drives," organised by van der Venter and Sir Duncan Mackenzie, collected its remnants at their leisure. It was fortunate for the British cause, for a far more formidable rebellion under abler soldiers than Maritz was now threatening in the very heart of the Union.

The situation in East Africa in the first months of war was the gravest which a British colony had to face. The German province was rich, well-organised, and strategically well-situated, for our Uganda railway, which formed the sole communications between Uganda, the East African plateau, and the sea, ran parallel with the northern frontier at a distance of from fifty to one hundred miles, and offered a natural and easy object of attack. There is reason to believe that the German scheme of operations, while providing for invasions of Nyassaland, North-East Rhodesia, and the British shores of Victoria Nyanza, aimed especially at an advance by land against Mombasa and the railway, which should be assisted by the *Koenigsberg* from the sea.

The size of the German forces is hard to estimate. Lord Crewe, in the House of Lords, spoke of native infantry and police to the number of 2,000; but there is little doubt that the native levies were at least 5,000, and that there were some 3,000 whites, recruited partly from the residents and partly from German reservists in the East, who had come thither by sea at the outbreak of war. The Germans got their native forces largely from the Sudan, which was the chief recruiting ground of the King's African Rifles; but they also enlisted the local tribesmen, especially the Masai and the Manyumwezi. They were especially strong in machine-guns, of which they had four to each company.

The British forces at the start were almost non-existent. In British East Africa and Uganda, they consisted of the 3rd and 4th battalions of the King's African Rifles, numbering under 1,000. These troops were mainly stationed on the northern frontier and in Jubaland, where a punitive expedition had just been dispatched against some of the Somali and Abyssinian tribes. All companies were at once recalled, and about 500 King's African Rifles were concentrated. Some 200 police were obtained for the defence of the railway line, by means of calling out the reserves and weakening police posts wherever possible.

Two volunteer corps were raised among the white settlers—the

East African Mounted Rifles and the East African Regiment. The latter was a failure, and never reached a higher figure than 50, but the former was nearly 400 strong. The existing Uganda Railway Volunteers—less than 100—were also called out, and employed in guarding bridges. As time went on further volunteer units were raised from Indian residents. A small body of Somali scouts was created, and a number of Arabs were recruited by Captain Wavell, one of the few Englishmen who have made the pilgrimage to Mecca. In Nyassaland and North-East Rhodesia there were small bodies of police, aided by white volunteers.

The total British defence force, therefore, in the first three weeks of war may be put at under 1,200, much of it of doubtful quality. The King's African Rifles were first-class fighting men, and the new Mounted Rifles, recruited from young British settlers of good blood and from the Boers of Uasin Gishu, were a force whose members reached a remarkable standard of shooting and *veldcraft*. But it is difficult to believe that so small an army could have made a serious stand if the Germans had pushed their northern invasion with vigour. For some obscure reason Germany did little in this direction during August, but contented herself with attacks on the south and west borders.

On 13th August the campaign began by an attack of a British cruiser on the German capital, Dar-es-Salam. The port was bombarded, and landing parties made their way into the harbour and completely destroyed the new wireless installation. They finished their work by dismantling the German ships, and by sinking the floating dock and the *Moewe*, a survey ship of 650 tons. On the same day, on Lake Nyassa, the British steamer *Gwendolen* surprised the German steamer *Von Wissmann* at Sphinxhaven on the eastern shore, took her crew and captain prisoners, and rendered her helpless. Three weeks later two vigorous attacks were made in the south-west.

At Karongwa, one of the chief British ports on Lake Nyassa, a small garrison of 50 was attacked by a force of 400, but held on long enough for supports to arrive. These supports decisively defeated the invaders, and drove them over the border with the loss of half their white officers. The second attack was made upon Abercorn in North-East Rhodesia, just south of Lake Tanganyika. A body of Rhodesian police drove it back, and captured a field-gun. Fighting continued intermittently all along this part of the frontier, but the balance leaned heavily in the British favour. Germany was keeping her best troops for her northern campaign.

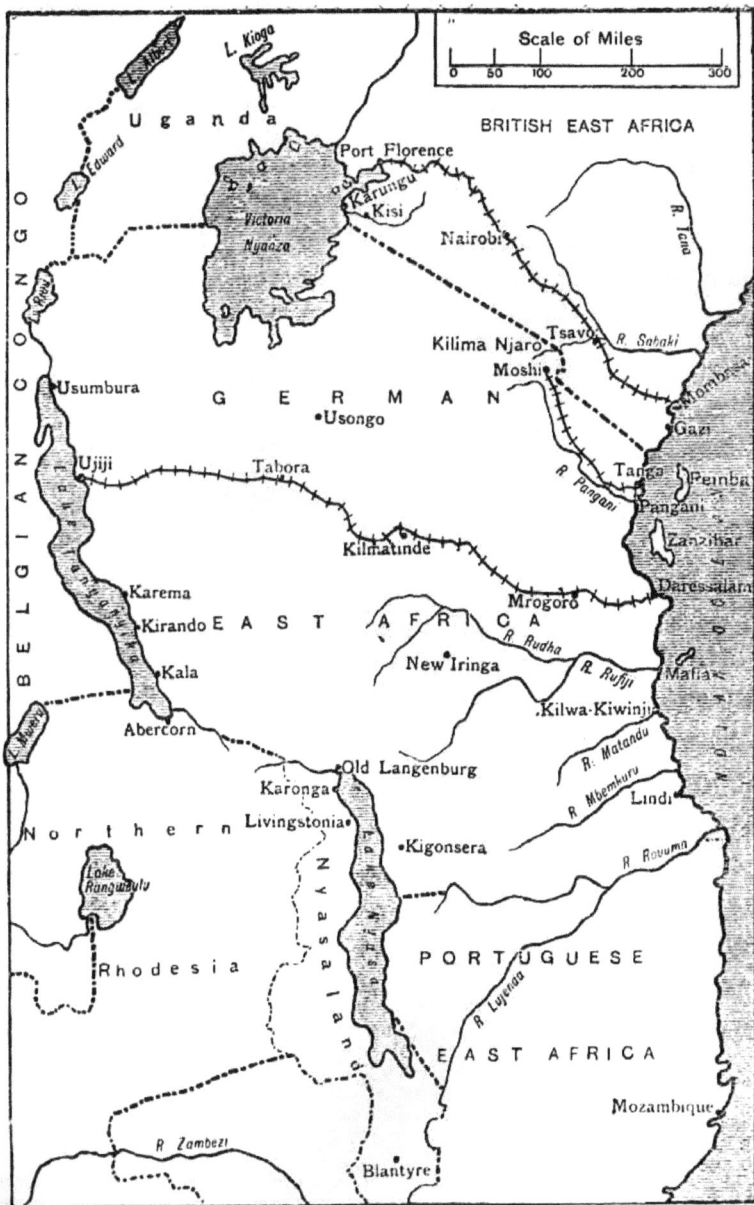

German East Africa.

On 3rd September reinforcements arrived for the British. Briga-dier-General J. M. Stewart reached Nairobi and assumed command of all the British troops. He brought with him the 29th Punjabis, a battal-ion of Imperial Service troops, one battery of Calcutta Volunteer Ar-tillery, one battery of Maxim guns, and one mountain battery. He had come only just in time, for the Germans were beginning operations against the Uganda railway. About 20th August they had seized the small frontier post of Taveta under Kilimanjaro, which was in danger-ous proximity to their chief northern military post of Moschi. They had also taken the frontier post of Vanga, on the coast, due south from Mombasa. Early in September they sent a detachment to blow up the Uganda railway at Maungu.

The history of this expedition is curious. They arrived comfort-ably within twenty miles of the line, guided by the excellent German maps. There, however, the maps stopped, and they were compelled to have recourse to English ones. The result was that they missed the water-holes, went eight miles out of their course, and were captured to a man. Thus, may the deficiencies of a Survey Department prove an asset in war.

A more serious advance was made on 6th September, when a force of Germans, about 600 strong, marched down the Tsavo River. They were much delayed by Lieutenant Hardingham with a mounted in-fantry company of King's African Rifles, who harassed them day and night, and gave time for a half battalion of the 29th Punjabis and several companies of the King's African Rifles to come up. An engage-ment was fought about five miles from the Tsavo railway bridge, and the enemy were driven back in some confusion. This success enabled the establishment of advance posts at Mzima and Campiya Marabu, which managed to maintain their position against repeated German assaults.

Three days later, on 10th September, the northern frontier was crossed at its extreme western end. The Germans occupied the fron-tier town of Kisi, near the Victoria Nyanza. On the 12th two com-panies of King's African Rifles, with two Maxims and some native police, surprised this force, who retired in disorder upon the lake port of Karungu. About the same time an action was fought on the lake itself. Two German *dhows* were sunk, and the British steamer *Winifred* sailed into Karungu Bay to relieve the town. At first it was driven off, but it returned with a colleague, the *Kavirondo*, and in the face of the British strength the Germans evacuated Karungu and fell back over

South African Commandos

the border.

During September there were other attacks on the northern frontier, making a total of seven in all, but much the most dangerous was the advance along the coast from Vanga towards Mombasa. The expedition was to be supported by the *Koenigsberg*, which was to shell the town and occupy the island, while the land forces were to destroy the bridge connecting Mombasa with the mainland. Something prevented the *Koenigsberg* from playing its part—perhaps the presence of British warships—but the land attack came very near succeeding. The Germans were 600 strong, with six machineguns, and they were met at Gazi by Captain Wavell's Arab company, strengthened by some King's African Rifles from Jubaland. This little force held up the invaders for several days, and on 2nd October were reinforced by some Indian troops.

Gazi was a very fine performance, for practically all the European officers were wounded before help arrived, and the command of the King's African Rifles passed to a native colour-sergeant, who handled his men with great coolness and skill, and headed the charge which drove back the enemy. Towards the end of October, the German attacks slackened, and the position resolved itself into a stalemate. The British troops remained on the defensive, waiting until a big Indian contingent should arrive in the beginning of November. The Germans occupied British territory at Taveta and at Longido on the Romba River, and they had an advance post between the Romba and the Tsavo.

The defence had had great luck, but had on the whole acquitted itself well. In such a campaign the attackers had to fight against the country as well as against human opponents. All along the northern border the waterless desert is covered with thorny scrub, which makes military operations desperately difficult. At a time when soldiers elsewhere were shivering in the mud of the Aisne, the East African force had to contend with intolerable heat and thirst. Much of the country was wholly virgin; there were no maps or roads; and wild beasts made picketing and scouting a sensational task. Happily, most of the men engaged in the work were familiar with the conditions. Most of the officers had hunted big game over a similar country, and the African levies were bush-bred and expert *shikaris*.

One officer's letter ran:

This is an awful country to fight in, and an ideal one for way-

SCHUTZTRUPPE FIRING BATTERY GUN

laying. It is one mass of bush and thorny scrub, in which you can walk right on to the enemy without being seen. Last night they put me out on picket duty on the hills. I got a grand view of Kilimanjaro in the moonlight—it looked awfully fine with its snowy peak; but really the job was a nervy one, considering that the place was teeming with rhino and lion, and we had to stand in the open without even a fire. The lions could be heard roaring quite close by, and besides that many other sounds of animal life could be heard. All this is very nice, but awe-inspiring.

CHAPTER 2

The South African Rebellion

The grant of self-government to the Transvaal and Orange Free State in 1906, four years after the conclusion of the South African War, was a bold step, which occasioned much uneasiness to those who were most familiar with the temper of the backveld. A strong people like the Boers do not surrender readily their dreams, and their tenacity of purpose was kept alive by certain sections of the Dutch Church, and by the ignorance and remoteness from modern life of the rural population. That the venture did not end in disaster was due to two events which could not have been foreseen. One was the movement towards a Union of South Africa, the foundations of which had been laid by Lord Milner's reconstruction after the war, and which Lord Selborne, aided by a brilliant band of young Englishmen, brought to a successful conclusion. The second was the appearance of two Dutch statesmen of the first quality.

The old Afrikander leaders, like Mr. Hofmeyer, had often been men of great ability and foresight, but they had lacked the accommodating temper of statesmanship. General Botha, the first Prime Minister of the Union, had been the ablest of the Boer generals, and his subsequent work entitles him to a high place among Imperial statesmen. He had the large simplicity of character and the natural magnetism which makes the born leader of men; his record in the field gave him the devoted allegiance of the old commandos; he was a sincere patriot, both of South Africa and of the Empire, for, while abating nothing of his loyalty towards the land of his birth, he saw that the fortunes of South Africa were bound up inextricably with the fortunes of the Empire as a whole; while he had that noble opportunism, that wide practical sagacity, which enabled him to move by slow degrees and to conciliate divergent interests by sheer tact and goodwill.

His lieutenant, General Smuts, had won fame alike as a scholar, a lawyer, and a commander in the field. With greater knowledge and a keener intellect than his chief, he had not General Botha's gift of popularity and popular leadership; but between them the two showed a combination of talents which it would be hard to parallel from any other part of the British dominions.

General Botha had not an easy part to play. The Unionist Party, led first by Sir Starr Jameson and then by Sir Thomas Smartt, while remaining the official Opposition, might be trusted to cooperate in all reasonable legislation. But among the Dutch there was a section, led by General Herzog, and drawing its support chiefly from the Orange Free State, which was definitely anti-British, and aimed not at racial union but at Dutch ascendancy. It was a true party of reaction, narrow and sectional in its aims, and bitter in its spirit. There was also growing up on the Rand and in the industrial centres a Labour Party, largely officered by professional agitators from overseas, which realised the delicacy of South African economic conditions, and aimed at a "hold-up" in the interests of a class.

It will thus be seen that South African politics showed few affinities with those of other British countries. The party in power, General Botha's, was a Conservative Party, composed mainly of landowners and farmers, and representing landed capital; the Opposition, mainly British in blood, contained most of the industrial capitalists, and was mildly progressive in character; the Labour Party was not such as we are familiar with in Britain, but in the main rigidly "class" in its aims and anarchical in its methods; while the Herzogites were nakedly reactionary and obscurantist. As usually happens, the two extremes tended to form a working alliance, and we had the extraordinary spectacle of the Rand agitator and the *taakhaar* from the wilds meeting on the same platform.

General Botha before the war began had cleared the air by two bold steps. He had dismissed General Herzog from the Ministry, and definitely dissociated himself from his aims, thereby driving the Herzogites into violent opposition. Then he had dealt faithfully with the Labour Party. The first great strike on the Rand in 1913 had been a success, for the Government were unprepared, and the strike leaders dictated their own terms. The second attempt was a complete fiasco. The Government called out all its forces, the reign of terror was broken in three days, and ten of the leaders were summarily deported under martial law. The result was to bring the official Opposition much closer to the Government, but to array against the Prime Minister a dangerous faction made up of the Herzogites and the defeated and discredited Labour Party.

The advent of war made a new division. General Herzog found that he could not collect a following, and became a trimmer. He attacked the Government, but forbore to aid the rebels when the insurrection broke out. The Labour Party, considering their treatment, behaved with genuine patriotism; many of their leaders took service in the new army, the working men of the Rand hastened to enlist, and General Botha's rescinding of the deportation order was a fitting recognition of this loyalty. But meantime a very serious falling away was becoming apparent in the ranks of the Dutch. It cut across political parties, for many of the Herzogites supported General Botha's policy, and intriguers were busy among those who had never followed Herzog.

The great mass of the Dutch people never wavered. Maritz's performance had offended many who would otherwise have been lukewarm on the British side, for he had in effect invaded the Cape province with foreign troops. But in certain districts a general discontent with the trend of modern politics, and dark memories of the South African War, combined with religious fanaticism to produce a dangerous temper. Presently treason found its leaders.

In the last war there was a certain *predikant* of Lichtenburg, Van Rensburg by name, who acquired a great reputation for second sight. He used to be known to our Intelligence Department as "Delarey's prophet," and was supposed to have much influence over that distinguished general. After peace he went on living in Lichtenburg, and that influence increased, while his reputation spread far and wide through the back-*veld*. When war with Germany broke out he discovered that the events foretold in the *Book of Revelation* were at hand, and that Germany was the agent appointed of God to purify the world.

If we dared to draw the sword upon her he prophesied the blackest sorrows. He had a number of visions, one of red and blue and black bulls, and one of an angel perched on the Paardekraal monument, which he interpreted on the same lines. The disaster at Hex River on 11th September to the troop-train carrying the Kaffrarian Rifles seemed to the superstitious a vindication of his forecast. Four days later came a second instalment. The prophet had an eye to local politics, and had announced that Generals Delarey, Beyers, and De Wet were the leaders destined to restore the old Republic.

Christiaan de Wet

On the night of 15th September Generals Delarey and Beyers were travelling in a motorcar westward from Johannesburg, and were challenged by a police patrol which was on the look-out for a gang of desperadoes. Beyers bade the car drive on, probably fearing that his plot had been betrayed, and a shot was fired which ricocheted and killed Delarey. The true story of that night and of Delarey's intentions is still untold. It may be that he had been won over to rebellion, but it is difficult for those who shared the friendship of that high-minded gentleman to believe that he would have brought himself to violate the oath of allegiance which he had taken to the British Crown.

About Beyers's disloyalty there was soon little doubt. Early in September he had resigned his post as Commandant-General of the Union Defence Force, in a letter which revealed more than he intended, and to which General Smuts most effectively replied. He had done brilliant work in the Zoutpansberg during the South African War, and probably ranked next after Generals Botha, Delarey, and Smuts among the Dutch commanders. But for some time, German agents had been working upon his vanity, while the "Prophet" played upon his sombre religion. He had visited Germany, and been received by the Emperor, and from that honour he had never recovered.

We need not judge him too hardly, for he paid the penalty of his folly; and it would be unreasonable to expect that rebellion would seem a heinous crime to one who, twelve years before, had been fighting against Britain. The real gravamen of his offence is that he broke the military oath which he had sworn as Commandant-General. Along with General Kemp, a former lieutenant of Delarey's and a good soldier, he proceeded to stir up disaffection in the Western Transvaal. With him was joined the famous Christian de Wet, whose name was at one time a household word.

De Wet was not a general of the calibre of Botha, Smuts, and Delarey, and his chronic lack of discipline spoiled more than one of the last-named's movements. But as a guerilla fighter in his own countryside he had no equal. He had not Delarey's moral dignity or Beyers's knowledge of modern conditions, being a Boer of the old, stiff, narrow, back-veld type, with a strong vein of religious fanaticism. But his name was one to conjure with, and his accession to the ranks of the irreconcilables vastly increased the difficulty of the Government's problem.

The main strength of the movement lay in the "*bywoner*," or squatter class, the "poor whites" who had been created by the Boer system

Union Cavalry

of large farms and large families. For them the future held no hope. In the old days they had staffed the various treks into the wilderness, but outlets were closing, and Africa was filling up. They had little education or intelligence, but they had enough to know that their economic position was growing desperate, and they not unnaturally struck for revolution when the chance came. They made up the bulk of De Wet's men, and the rest were a few religious fanatics, a few Republican theorists, some men who still cherished bitter memories of the late war, and a number of social *déclassés* and unsuccessful politicians. Little pity need be wasted on the latter, but it is not easy to withhold a certain sympathy for the luckless "*bywoner*," for whom the world had no longer a place.

The rebellion was not long in revealing itself. On 26th October the Union Government announced that De Wet was busy commandeering *burghers* in the north of the Orange Free State, while Beyers was at the same task in the Western Transvaal. On the 24th De Wet seized Heilbron, a little town in the north Free State, on a branch of the main line from Cape Town to Pretoria. Further, at Reitz, he had stopped a train and arrested some Union soldiers who were travelling by it. Beyers, meantime, with a commando formed chiefly of Delarey's old soldiers, was in Rustenburg, threatening Pretoria.

General Botha at once summoned the *burghers* to put down the revolt, and to their eternal honour they responded willingly. It was no easy decision for many of them. They were called on to fight against men of their own blood, some of whom had been their comrades or their leaders in the last war. From farm to farm went the summons, and many a farmer took down his Mauser, which had shot nothing but buck since Diamond Hill or Colesberg, and up-saddled his pony, as he had done before the great Sand River concentration. The magic name of Botha did not fail in its appeal, and in a few weeks, he had over 30,000 under arms. He was now a man of fifty-two years of age, tired with heavy years of office and a sedentary life, and not in the best of health. The rebellion must have been peculiarly bitter to one who had striven beyond all others for a united South African people, and who was not likely to forget the friendships of the old strenuous days.

He did not suffer the grass to grow under his feet. Resolving to clear Beyers out of the neighbourhood of the capital before he turned to deal with De Wet, he entrained for Rustenburg on the 26th, and fell in with the enemy next day to the south of that town, about eighty miles from Pretoria, where the Zeerust road goes through the north-

De Wet during the Rebellion

ern foothills of the Magaliesberg. There he smote Beyers and Kemp so fiercely that their commandos were scattered, eighty prisoners were taken, and the leaders fled incontinently to the south-west. Part of the rebel forces went northward into the hills of Waterberg, but the bulk of them followed their generals to Lichtenburg.

In Lichtenburg Colonel Alberts was waiting for them. His first encounter was unfortunate, for no of his men were cut off from the rest, and captured at Treurfontein by the rebels. A day or two later he retrieved the disaster, recovered the prisoners, and thoroughly beat Claasen, the rebel leader. Meanwhile that portion of Beyers's force which had gone north to Waterberg, and which seems to have been under the command of Muller, was busied in raiding the line that runs north from Pretoria, till Colonel van der Venter, fresh from his success in the Cape, hustled it back into the hills. On 8th November he caught the raiders at Sandfontein, near Warmbaths, some sixty miles from Pretoria, and dispersed them, with many killed, wounded, and prisoners. The remnants fled back to Rustenburg and the west.

By this time, we had news of the whereabouts of Beyers and Kemp. Hunted by Colonel Lemmer, the former fled south-west to the flats of Bloemhof, crossed the Vaal River, and entered the Orange Free State. He had a sharp fight near the junction of the Vaal and the Vet, and lost about 400, as well as most of his transport, but succeeded himself in getting clear away. The men whom Colonel Alberts had already beaten were now with Kemp making for Bechuanaland and German territory. They were safe enough in that direction, for the Kalahari Desert at the end of the dry season might be trusted to take its toll of rash adventurers. On 7th November General Smuts made a speech in Johannesburg, in which, summing up the situation, he announced that the rebellion in the Cape was over, that the Transvaal rebels were now only a few scattered bands, and that in the Orange Free State alone, where De Wet was at work, had the revolt assumed any serious proportions.

De Wet had only a month of freedom, but he made good use of it so far as concerned the distance covered. Ten years before he would have made a very different sort of fight among those flats and *kopjes* of the northern Free State, where spring was beginning to tinge with green the long umber and yellow distances. But now the stars in their courses fought against him. His own countrymen had become prudent, and did not see the admirable joke of *sjamboking* a magistrate who had once fined him five shillings for whipping a native. They

LANDINGS AT TANGA

Askaris skirmishing at Tanga

gave information to the Government, and grudged ammunition and stores to the good cause.

Once he had had fine sport in that district, slipping through block-house lines and eluding the clumsy British columns, but now he found himself being constantly brought up against that accursed thing, modern science. So long as he could trust to a good horse matters went well, but what was he to do when his pursuers took to motor-cars which covered twenty miles where the British Mounted Infantry used to cover five? The times were out of joint for De Wet, and so he went *sjamboking* and commandeering through the land, perpetually losing his temper, and delivering bitter philippics against these latter days.

General Botha was "ungodly," the English were "pestilential," Maritz was the only true man. Heresy, Imperialism, and negrophilism were jumbled together as the enemy. "King Edward," he cried, with some pathos, "promised to protect us, but he did not keep his promise, and allowed a magistrate to be put over us." There you have the last cry of the *ancien régime* in South Africa, which saw patriarchalism and personal government vanishing from a machine, made world.

De Wet was at Vrede on 28th October, when he had the famous interview with the magistrate already referred to. Meanwhile his lieu-tenant, Wessels, had looted Harrismith, near the Natal border, and damaged the railway line. Thereafter De Wet turned west, and found sanctuary in the neighbourhood of Winburg, where, on 7th Novem-ber, at a place called Doornberg, he defeated a Union force under Commander Cronje, and lost his son David, At the time his army seems to have numbered 2,000 men. Next day a second rebel force was beaten at Kroonstadt by Colonel Manie Botha, who continued the pursuit for several days.

By this time General Botha, having pretty well cleared the Trans-vaal, was on his way south, and on the 11th came in touch with De Wet at Marquard, about twenty miles east of Winburg. The rebels were in four bodies, one at Marquard, one at a place called Bantry, a third at Hoenderkop, and a fourth, with which was De Wet himself, in the Mushroom Valley. General Botha's plan was to surround the whole rebel force, two Union armies, under Colonels Brits and Lukin, work-ing round its flanks. Something went wrong, however, with the timing of the movement, the dispatches miscarried, and Lukin and Brits did not reach their allotted posts in time. In spite of this accident, De Wet was completely defeated. General Botha took 282 prisoners, released

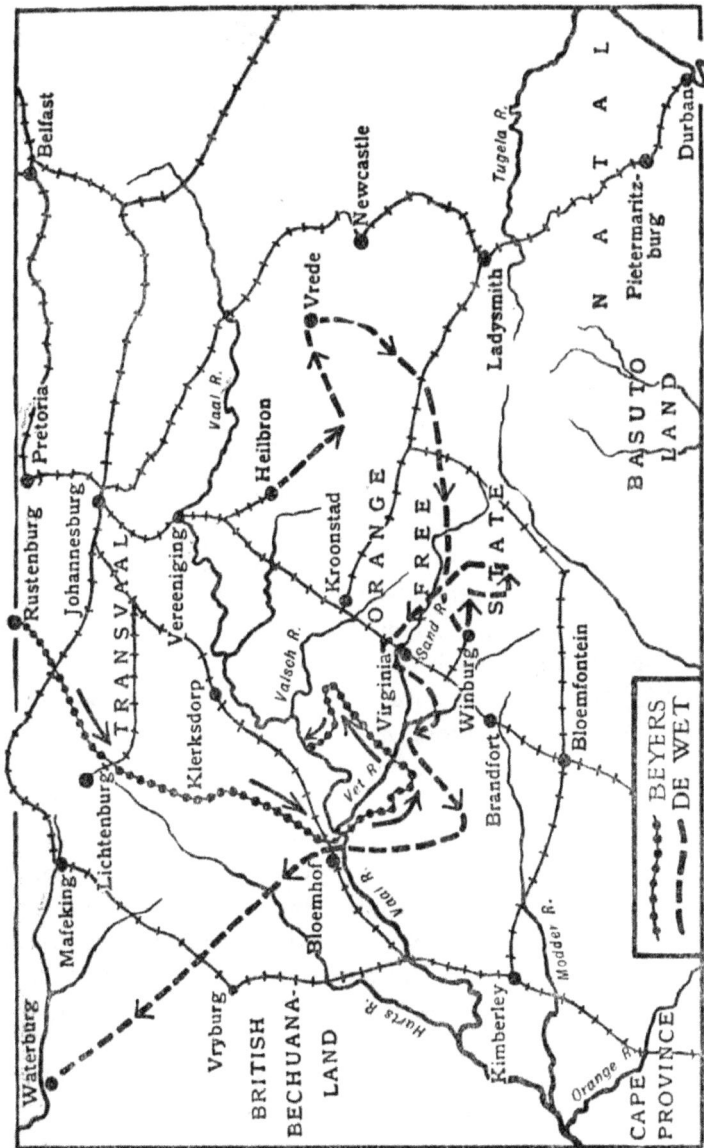

Map illustrating the wanderings of De Wet and Beyers.

most of the loyalists taken by the rebels, and captured a large quantity of transport. On the 13th, it was officially announced that the interrupted train service between Bloemfontein and Johannesburg would be resumed.

De Wet at first fled south, but presently doubled back, and on the 16th was at Virginia, on the main line. Two armoured trains on the railway managed to prevent a large part of the rebel force from crossing, and to head it eastward. Presently some of its commandants began to come in, and many who had taken up arms, attracted by the clemency of General Botha's proclamation, laid them down again. De Wet was aiming at a junction with Beyers, who was in the Hoopstad district at the time. Beyers, however, was in trouble on his own account.

On the 15th, Colonel Celliers had fallen upon him at Bultfontein, and had beaten him thoroughly, and made large captures. Most of the 1,500 rebels were driven northwards, many across the Vaal. Accordingly, De Wet, fleeing from Virginia down the Sand and Vet Rivers, found Celliers ahead of him, and heard of Beyers's disaster. He saw that the game was up, and halted his force near Boshof. There seems to have been considerable disaffection in its ranks, and in a final address to them he advised all who were tired of fighting to hide their rifles and go home. Many took the advice, including two of his sons, many yielded themselves to the Union forces, but De Wet himself, with twenty-five men, made one last dash for liberty.

On 21st November he tried to cross the Vaal, and was driven back by Commandant Dutoit. In the evening, however, with a following now reduced to six, he managed to slip over the river above Bloemhof, and took the road for Vryburg and the north-west. He now picked up some fugitives, and the small commando crossed the railway line to Rhodesia, twenty miles north of Vryburg. He had, apparently, conceived the bold scheme of going through the Kalahari to German South-West Africa. But he had not allowed for the motorcars of his pursuers. For a day or two there was heavy rain, which made the roads bad, and gave the Boer ponies of his party an advantage over any motor.

But by the 27th the weather had cleared, the *veld* was hard and dry, and Colonel Brits, who had taken up the chase, began to capture the slower members of the commando. As the fugitives penetrated into the western desert their case became more hopeless. De Wet was forced by the motors behind him to cover fifty miles at a stretch without off-saddling, a thing hateful to the Boer horse-master. The

MARITZ COUMN AT UPINGTON 1914

end came on 1st December, when, at a farm called Waterburg, about a hundred miles west of Mafeking, De Wet and his handful surrendered to Colonel Jordaan. He was taken to Vryburg, and two days later entered Johannesburg a prisoner. He had yielded at the end with a shaggy good humour. Having decided that modern conditions were the devil, he was glad to see his own Afrikanders such adepts at the use of the powers of darkness.

With the capture of De Wet the rebellion was virtually at an end. There was a good deal of skirmishing along the south and north banks of the lower Vaal. Kemp, accompanied by the Lichtenburg "Prophet," fled west after Treurfontein to the little town of Schweizer Reneke, and thence towards Vryburg. He had some fighting at Kuruman, from which he headed south-west across the Southern Kalahari. He was engaged again north of Upington, and it was a very battered remnant which ultimately crossed the border of German South-West Africa. Early in December General Botha organised a great sweeping movement from Reitz, which ended in the surrender of Wessels with the only large body of rebels still in the field.

Beyers, with a small commando, after his defeat at Bultfontein had haunted the southern shore of the Vaal between Hoopstad and Kroonstad. On the morning of 8th December he fell in with a body of Union troops under Captain Uys, and was driven towards the river. He and some companions endeavoured to cross the Vaal, which was in high flood, and, midway in the stream, he found his horse failing, and slipped from its back to swim. His greatcoat hampered him, and he tried in vain to get rid of it. A companion heard him cry, "*Ik kan nie meer nie*" (I can do no more), as he disappeared. His body was found two days later. He had been drowned, for there was no bullet mark on him.

By the end of December, the last embers of disaffection had been stamped out within the Union territory. Of the five leaders whom Maritz had named, De Wet was captured, Muller was wounded and a prisoner, Beyers was dead, Kemp was across the German border, and Herzog had never declared himself. In less than two months General Botha had harried the rebels round the points of the compass, and had taken 7,000 of them prisoners, with a total casualty list to the Union Army of no more than 334. He exhibited great magnanimity and wisdom in his hour of triumph. Rebels who had been members of the Defence Force and had broken their military oath were very properly put on trial for their life.

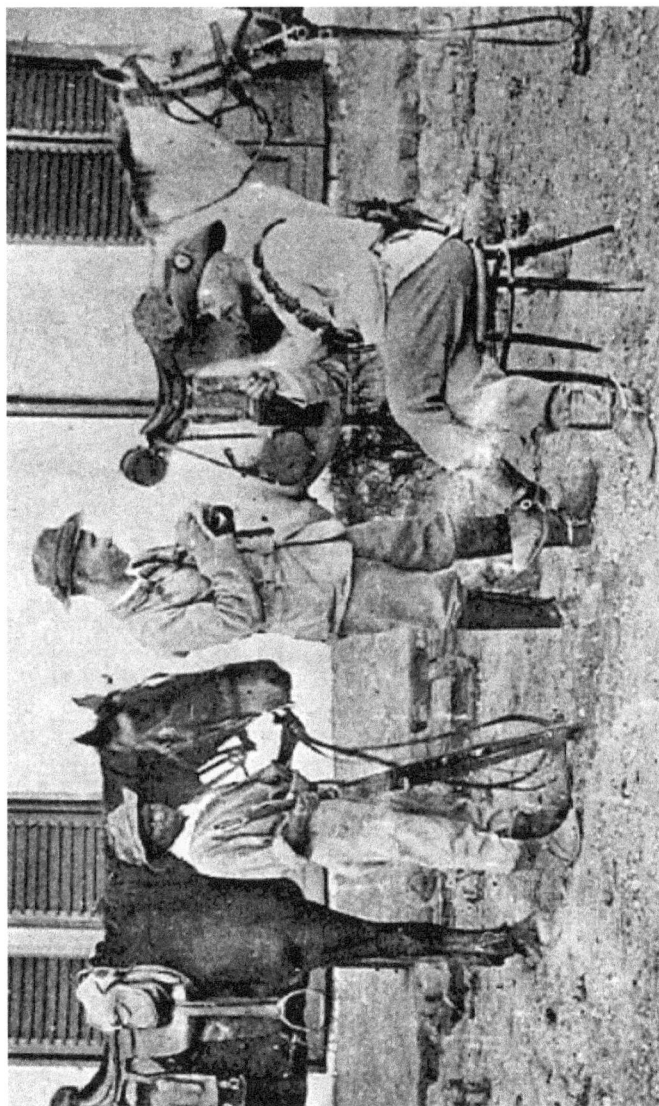

MARITZ AT UPINGTON

But to the rank and file he showed no harshness, and, in the interests of South Africa's future, this clemency was not misplaced. Rebellion could not, for the country Boers, carry the moral stigma which it would bear if dabbled in by an ordinary Briton. The Empire had no sentimental claim upon them, and the case for loyalty founded on material interests required a certain level of education before it could be understood. Besides, so far as the older race of Boers was concerned, insurrection was in their bones; it had always been a recognised political expedient, and, indeed, for more than a century had been the national pastime.

There is little to tell of the rest of the fighting in Africa till the end of the year. Togoland was quiescent in our hands. In the Cameroons the French and British were slowly pushing the Germans farther into the interior, while on all the northern border there was a succession of raids and counter-raids. The Germans seem to have hoped much from a Panislamic propaganda among the Mohammedan natives, but the entry of Turkey into the war made no difference in West Africa, where the *Khalif* has never been a name to conjure with. The campaign in South-West Africa had to wait till General Botha had his hands free of local rebellion. But the last months of 1914 showed a certain activity in East Africa.

In that country, as we have seen, we were compelled by the weakness of our resources to stand on the defensive, a role in which, by a mixture of skill and good fortune, we had reasonable success. But with the beginning of November our forces were largely increased, and we began a forward movement which ended in a real disaster.

On 1st November a second Indian Expeditionary Force arrived on the East African coast. It was commanded by Major-General Aitken, and consisted of one British battalion—the 1st Loyal North Lancashires, the 95th and 101st Indian regiments, the 61st King George's Own Pioneers, the 1st Palamcotta Light Infantry, the 1st Kashmir Rifles, together with a few other detachments of Imperial Service troops, accompanied by two mountain batteries. On the morning of 2nd November this force, escorted by two gunboats, lay off the German port of Tanga, the coast terminus of the Moschi railway, and summoned it to surrender.

The officer in charge asked for some hours' grace in order that he might communicate with the governor, who was then absent. This was granted, and the original time was largely extended, and used by the Germans to hurry down every available soldier by the Moschi

Vreikorps, South African Rebels

line. Towards evening the British general grew impatient, and landed one and a half battalions, who advanced through the coast scrub towards the town. There it was apparent that a strong defence had been prepared, and the invaders had to fall back towards the shore, where they could be covered by the gunboats.

The next day was occupied in landing the rest of the force, and the attack was renewed on the morning of the 4th. It proved a complete failure. The Germans had mastered the art of bush fighting. Ropes were hidden under the sand of the paths, and, when stepped on, brought down flags which gave the enemy the required range. They also adopted an old Manyumwezi trick, and hid hives of bees half-stifled with smoke beside the roads, which swarmed out when the lids were twitched off by concealed wires, and grievously stung our men. One of the North Lancashires had over a hundred stings extracted.

Yet we managed to reach the town of Tanga, where the 101st Grenadiers attacked on the left with the bayonet, and the Kashmir Rifles and the North Lancashires effected an entrance on the right. There we met a deadly enfilading fire from the housetops, and were forced back with heavy losses. There was nothing for it but to retire to the coast and re-embark. Our casualties were nearly 800, and included 141 British officers and men, so that the Tanga reverse was the most costly of the minor African battles. General Aitken's force went north to the East African Plateau, where it continued during the next months to act as a garrison and watch the borders.

BATTLE OF TANGA

CHAPTER 3

The African Theatre of War, 1915

The African theatre of war during the first four months of the new year had little of interest except in the extreme south-west, where General Botha was slowly and patiently forcing his way to the German capital. In Egypt, after the fiasco of the Canal attack in February, there were only affairs of outposts. On 22nd February the French cruiser *Desaix* landed marines at Akaba, and her guns cleared the Turkish troops from the town.

On 31st March a British cruiser bombarded Mowilah, another place at the head of the Red Sea. Patrols and aircraft along the Suez Canal reported that the nearest enemy posts were four days' march distant, and from other sources we learned that their main army was still quartered in Palestine. But on 22nd March there was another attempt to force the Canal. An enemy force, mainly infantry with guns, but including a few cavalry squadrons, was located near El Kubri, in the neighbourhood of Suez. Shots were exchanged, and the Turks retired to a point eight miles from the Canal.

Next day the British, under Lieutenant-General Sir George Younghusband, fell upon their camp and drove them to Nakhl, seventy miles inside the desert. A few stray Turks still haunted the Canal banks, and on 8th April shots were exchanged between patrols close to El Kantara. A few days later the French warship *St. Louis*, assisted by several hydroplanes, bombarded a large Turkish camp near Gaza. Camps were bombarded during the month at El Arish and El Sirr, and the Bikanir Camel Corps on 28th April had a brisk skirmish with a detachment of the enemy.

These, however, were minor incidents: it was clear that the Turkish Army destined for the invasion of the Canal was thoroughly impotent and disheartened; and Egypt was used as a base for our Dardanelles

GERMAN INFANTRY

operations without any anxiety as to its eastern frontiers.

THE CAMEROONS

In October the British left the Germans in the Cameroons reduced to defensive warfare in a difficult hinterland. The Allies were not slow to push their advantage. Presently two columns of the Anglo-French force, under Brigadier-General Dobell, were moving along the two lines of railway which run from Duala to the interior. The bulk of the troops were French Colonial infantry, under Colonel Mayer. Edea, a point on the railway and the Sanaga River some fifty miles from Duala, was the first object of attack, and it was arranged that it should be assailed both by parties moving on the railway and by parties ascending the river in boats. The march was difficult, moving through dense forests and much harassed by snipers; but there was no resistance in the town itself, which was occupied on 26th October. The enemy retired to Yaunde, a station far up on the interior plateau.

Six weeks later the Germans made an effort to regain Edea, but were beaten back with a loss of twenty Europeans and fifty-four natives. There followed an Allied advance in three columns against Yaunde, in which we fought two little battles on 27th and 28th January, and seized the post of Bersona. Colonel Mayer crossed the River Kele, and a British column a little farther north took the bridge of Ngua. Meanwhile north of Duala, on the other railway line, good progress had been made. During December we seized Nkongsamba and Baré, the latter a station six miles north of the railhead.

This gave us the whole of the northern line, and at Baré we made prizes of two aeroplanes which had not yet been unpacked. Our casualties were trifling, and our strict blockade of the coast meant that no recruits or supplies were available for the enemy. It was a form of campaign in which time was wholly on our side.

On the frontiers of the Cameroons there was a continuous war of skirmishes. To avenge our defeats at Garua and Nsanakong, a British force from Nigeria sailed to Ikom on the Cross River, crossed the border, and marched on Ossidinge, which was surrendered after a few shots. The French on their part sent in columns from their Chad Territories in the north and from French Equatoria on the east and south, so that the luckless defenders were surrounded by a ring of foes. It was a slow campaign, in a country of swamps and forests and equatorial heat, and there was no need of hurry, for haste only spelled disaster. The Allies had reproduced in miniature the siege conditions

SOUTH AFRICAN TROOPS CROSSING THE RIVER

which now prevailed in Europe.

EAST AFRICA

In East Africa our campaign was less prosperous. We left off the narrative on 4th November, when Major-General Aitken's force suffered disaster at Tanga, and was compelled to re-embark. To coincide with that movement an attack on Longido had been arranged, the fort in British territory north of Kilimanjaro which had been occupied by the Germans. This, too, was unsuccessful.

The East African Mounted Rifles and the Indian contingent detailed for the work were unable to capture a position held in superior strength and defended by many machine guns, and retired with considerable losses, including that gallant officer, Captain Sandbach of the 1st (Royal) Dragoons. Yet the attempt was not a total failure, for a few days later, on 17th November, the Germans quietly abandoned the place, and we promptly occupied it.

Then followed some isolated engagements. On 20th November a German force invaded Uganda, and, though repulsed at several points, forced the garrison to retire from Kyaka Fort, on the south bank of the River Kagera. Near Nguruman, there was an encounter between patrols, and all along the extended borders there were skirmishes of outposts. But it was not till the middle of January that we fought a battle and suffered our second serious disaster.

After their victory at Tanga the Germans had invaded our territory by the coast route; but with the assistance of naval forces we drove them back, and by the end of December we had cleared our borders and occupied the post of Jassin, twenty miles inside German territory, where there was a small sisal factory.

This was an advanced post, our real position being the valley of the Umba River to the north, and the town of Vanga at its mouth. Jassin was held by three companies of Indian infantry, and these were able to beat off a sudden German attack delivered on 12th January. Six days later, however, on 18th January, a powerful German force, at least 2,000 strong, with artillery and machine-guns, returned to the assault. Help was sent from the Umba valley, but it met with severe fighting on its way, and could not reach Jassin. On the morning of the 19th, the garrison, having expended all its ammunition, surrendered, and about 240 became prisoners of war.

The two British officers in command were congratulated by the German general on their gallant defence, and had their swords re-

A Schutztruppe

turned to them. A party of forty men of the Kashmir Rifles managed to fight their way through the enemy, and reached the British lines with a loss of half their number. The German success seems to have been due to their numerous machine guns, and their skill in using them. One of our machine-gun men, a native soldier of the King's African Rifles, succeeded in bringing his gun away. When he arrived at the main camp he reported himself, and apologized humbly for having left the tripod behind him. The German loss in the action was severe, for they had fifty-seven whites killed and wounded, including seven officers killed, heavy casualties among their native troops, and three machine guns smashed by our mountain batteries.

The disaster at Jassin compelled a withdrawal of our outlying posts in this region, and the Germans were justified in claiming that their East African territory was completely free from the enemy, while they held several posts inside the British borders. Our small successes were chiefly naval. Having taken the port of Shirati on the Victoria Nyanza, we used it as a base for our armed steamers, and on 6th March the *Winifred* drove ashore and totally disabled the *Muanza*, the only German armed steamer on the lake. On 8th January an expedition from Mombasa occupied the island of Mafia, off the mouth of the River Rufiji.

On 26th February we announced that from midnight on 28th February the coast of German East Africa would be blockaded, four days being allowed for the departure of neutral vessels. From that date the blockade of a coast line of over 300 miles was vigilantly kept up, and the German colony was placed in the same position as the Cameroons. Its armed forces might be strong, well equipped, and temporarily successful, but none the less they were the garrison of a beleaguered city.

SOUTH-WEST AFRICA

When General Botha declared war against German South-West Africa it was generally believed that his campaign would not be concluded before the great struggle in Europe had come to a decision. The strength of the Germans, and their ample provision of artillery, the immense distances to be covered, and the difficulties of reaching a decisive result in a country so strongly fortified by nature, inclined most men to the belief that the war would soon resolve itself into a stalemate and a siege. Such a view underrated the energy and the skill of the South African generals. So soon as the rebellion within

The East African Theatre.

Union territories had been finally crushed, General Botha set himself to carry out an admirable strategical plan against the German defence.

But, first, the last embers of the rebellion had to be extinguished. Moving along the Orange River, a body under Maritz and Kemp gained two small successes, surprising two posts at Langklip and Onydas held by the 8th Mounted Rifles. The arrival of reinforcements obliged them to abandon their prisoners and hastily retire. On 12th January Raman's Drift was retaken by Colonel Bouwer, which gave the Union force the entire line of the Orange, and penned the hostile remnants into the angle formed by the river and the German frontier.

On 24th January the rebels, dispirited and half starving, made their last sally. Led by Maritz and Kemp, and about 1,200 strong, they attacked Colonel Van der Venter at Upington, but they were easily repulsed. Next day the end came. The leaders offered to surrender unconditionally. On 3rd February Kemp and his commando—43 officers and 486 men, including the prophet Van Rensburg—surrendered at Upington, and some of Maritz's band followed suit at Kakamas. Maritz himself was not among them. Knowing that for him there would be no mercy, he fled back to German territory.

The position in January, when the main campaign against South-West Africa began, was as follows: We held Walfisch Bay and its surroundings, and on 14th January we seized without trouble the adjoining German port of Swakopmund, the terminus of the line to Windhoek and of the line to Tsumab and Grootfontein, in the north of the colony. We had held since September Luderitz Bay (or Angra Pequeña)—the terminus of the southern line which ran to Windhoek by Keetmanshoop. Our capture of Schuit Drift and Raman's Drift gave us the fords of the Orange. We therefore held all the gates of the German colony, and our command of the sea made us free to use them. General Botha's plan of campaign was an enveloping movement against Windhoek, and the forces at his disposal were divided into two main armies. The Northern, under his own command, was to move from Swakopmund as a base along the railway to Windhoek. The Southern, under General Smuts, was divided into three separate columns.

The first, under Sir Duncan Mackenzie, was directed to move east along the railway from Luderitz Bay. The second, under Colonel Van der Venter, was to move north along the line running from Warmbad to Keetmanshoop; while the third, under Colonel Berrange, was to start from Kimberley, and, crossing Bechuanaland, invade the colony

GERMAN SMALL ARTILLERY

from the east. All three columns were to concentrate at Keetman-shoop, whence, under Smuts, they would move northwards to join Botha. The plan was skilfully devised, for, if successful, it meant the shepherding of the German forces away from modern communications into the desert country of the eastern frontier, where the waterless sands of the Kalahari barred all escape.

Let us follow first the doings of the Northern army.

******

Note:—Botha's force consisted of the various Burgher commandos and volunteers. It had also the following units: Transvaal Scottish, 1st Rhodesian Regiment, Cape Town Highlanders, Kimberley Regiment, Rand Regiment, Rand Light Infantry, South African Irish, Northern Mounted Rifles, together with part of the Transvaal Horse Artillery and the South African Railway Engineers, who were employed in construction work.

******

During January the various bases were well provisioned, and from Swakopmund a railway was laid along the coast to Walfisch Bay, and sea walls built to facilitate landing. On 8th February, on his way from Cape Town, General Botha called at Luderitz Bay and reviewed Sir Duncan Mackenzie's troops at their camp forty-five miles from the coast. He reached Swakopmund on the 9th, and on the 22nd his army began to move. At first its progress was slow. Two German posts were seized without loss, and then nearly a month was spent in reconnoitring the enemy's strength and preparing an advanced base. On 19th March the business of clearing the railway was taken in hand.

That evening two mounted brigades left our post of Husab. The left column of the second brigade, under Colonel Celliers, had orders to cut the railway line between Jakalswater and Sphinx, and then, having hampered the movements of any reinforcements coming from Windhoek, to attack Jakalswater itself. The right column, under Colonel Alberts, was to seize Pforte, another station on the line. The first brigade, commanded by Colonel Brits, and accompanied by General Botha himself, was to attack Riet, an important point south of the railway, while the Bloemhof commando, operating on its flank, was directed to seize the hill of Schwarze Kopje.

The attack was timed for dawn on the 20th. Celliers, having cut the line and captured a train laden with supplies, moved against the German position at Jakalswater. There, however, he found the enemy strongly entrenched, and his attack failed in its main object, though it prevented assistance being sent to Pforte. At the latter place Alberts was wholly successful, and that afternoon received the surrender of the garrison—210 men and four guns. The main objective of the movement, however, was Riet, where the German position was very strong. Its right rested on the Swakop stream, its left on the foothills of the Langer Heinrichberg, while its guns, skilfully placed, commanded the main road and the river.

In our attack the gunners of the Transvaal Horse Artillery did admirable work, and so stoutly was it pressed that by the evening the enemy were driven out in disorder. A party of snipers, under Captain Lemmer, prevented the Germans from destroying the water-holes. The completeness of our success was marred only by the failure of the Bloemhof commando to reach its allotted place on the Schwarze Kopje, which would have enabled us to cut off the enemy's retreat.

During April the advance proceeded steadily. Colonel Skinner with the Kimberley regiment protected the railway behind us, and our control of the Tsumab line as far as Trekkopje prevented any serious operations against our left flank and rear. In the first days of May Botha with the main army at Kubas, and on the 5th, after a march of thirty-five miles, the junction of Karibib was reached and occupied. Another twenty miles took the army to Johann Albrechtshohe, and a further ten to Wilhelmstal. South of the railway runs the main road between Windhoek and the coast, and along this, too, our troops advanced. By this time all serious resistance was over for the Northern army. We must turn to the doings of General Smuts's army in the south.

The heaviest task fell to Van der Venter, moving north from the Orange.

He had with him the 1st South African Mounted Rifles (the old Cape Mounted Rifles), the 2nd S.A.M.R. (the old Natal Police), the 3rd S.A.M.R. (partly Natal Police and partly South African Constabulary), the 5th S.A.M.R. (part), the Witwatersrand Rifles, and the Transvaal Horse Artillery (part). The S.A.M.R. form the standing army of the Union.

He came into touch with the enemy at Nakob, and early in March he occupied Ukamas and other posts in that region. Ten miles north of Ukamas he seized the German camp at Nabas, with large quantities of stores, and thirty miles on occupied Platbeen. On 3rd April his left wing occupied the railway terminus of Warmbad, and in the following week he penetrated nearly a hundred miles north of it. On 11th

69

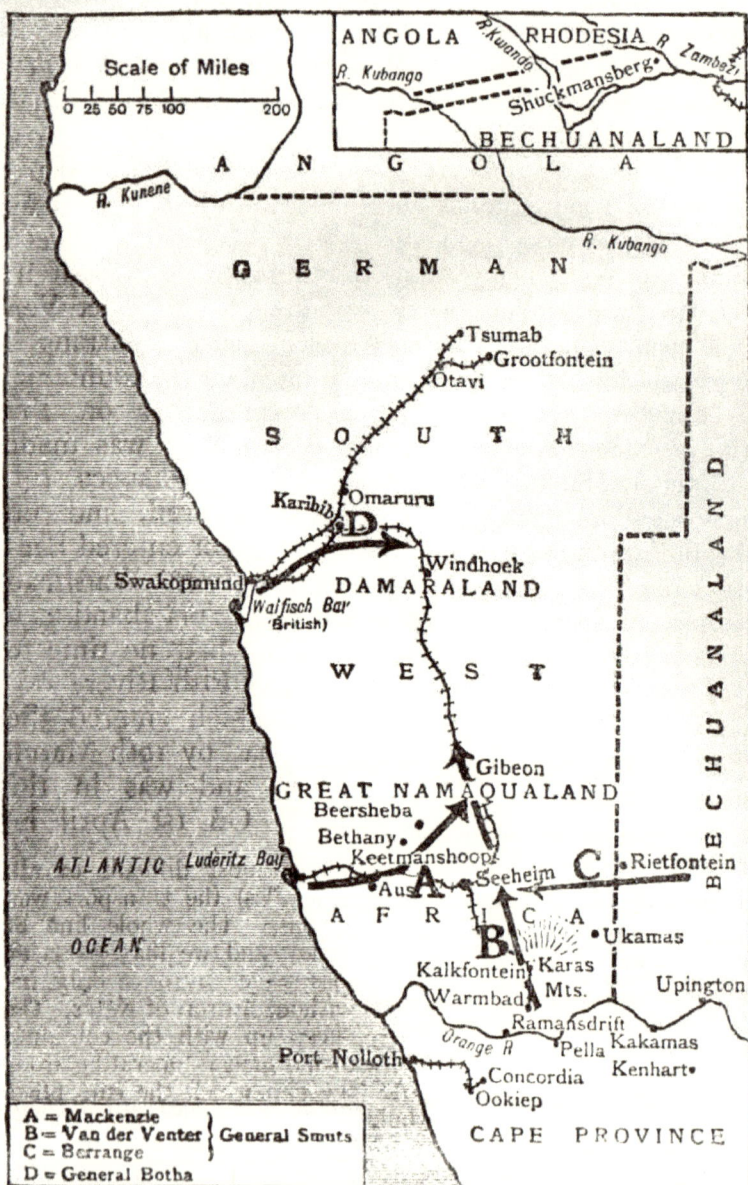

Map to illustrate the Capture of Windhoek.

April General Smuts met Van der Venter at Kalkfontein, and arranged to drive the enemy out of the Karas Mountains, which gave them an awkward position on the flanks of our advance.

The movement was made in three columns and was completely successful, the mountains were cleared, and on 17th April Van der Venter entered Seeheim, the junction of the lines from Warmbad and from Luderitz Bay. The Germans abandoned the place in such haste that they had no time to destroy the bridge across the Great Fish River.

Colonel Berrange's column, which entered the colony from the east, had by 19th March reached the borders, and was in the neighbourhood of Rietfontein.

His transport problem was the most difficult of all. From Kimberley to Kuruman (140 miles) the transport was by donkeys, and after that by oxen. The whole line of communication was about 600 miles, and we may guess at the difficulties of the 400 odd miles served by oxen only, including one stretch of in miles without a drop of water. Ox transport could not, of course, keep up with the columns, so the army was fed by a fleet of motorcars operating from the end of the line. At times the gap which the cars filled was over 40 miles. The whole affair was a very remarkable transport feat. After Berrange joined Van der Venter and Mackenzie, the eastern route was closed, and the whole Southern army was then supplied from Luderitz Bay.

On 1st April he captured an entrenched position at Hasuur, fifteen miles from the latter town. From there he fought his way westward, with constant skirmishes, to his appointed meeting-place with Van der Venter. The two forces met a little to the east of Keetmanshoop, in the third week of April.

Berrange had with him the 4th S.A.M.R. (the old S.A.C.), 5th S.A.M.R. (part), 1st Durban Light Infantry, 2nd Durban Light Infantry, 1st Kaffrarian Rifles, 2nd Kaffrarian Rifles, Queenstown Rifles, 1st City Rifles (Grahamstown), Bechuanaland Rifles, Imperial Light Horse, Brand's Horse, Enslin's Horse, Hartigan's Horse, Diamond Field Horse, together with part of the S.A. Railway Engineers, and the S.A. Motor Corps.

The combined column then advanced on Keetmanshoop, which surrendered without fighting on 2oth April. The place, which is 170 miles from Warmbad and 195 miles from Luderitz Bay, was the business capital of German Namaqualand, and its possession was highly advantageous. General Smuts made it his headquarters, and waited

German Transport Attacked

there for Mackenzie's force, which was moving inwards from Luderitz Bay.

Mackenzie had to begin by clearing the immediate neighbourhood of Luderitz Bay. Presently he seized Garub, seventy miles up the line, and advanced towards the hills which mark the end of the coastal desert. He occupied Aus, twenty miles farther on, where the Germans held a strongly fortified pass, from which they retired without a blow. There we had a hint of the new methods of warfare which about that time were coming into fashion in Flanders. Some of the wells were found to have been poisoned by arsenical sheep-dip, but happily the fact was discovered before our men could suffer by it. The thing had happened before in January near Swakopmund, and General Botha had sharply protested against this violation, not only of an article of The Hague Convention, to which Germany was a signatory, but of the fundamental decencies of war. The German commander replied that warning notices would be affixed to the poisoned wells, but this was clearly an evasion of the issue, and General Botha announced that he reserved the right to make reprisals for this barbarity.

At Aus Mackenzie's column was clear of the worst desert region. He left the railway, took Bethany, and struck north-east in the direction of Gibeon, a station on the line between Keetmanshoop and Windhoek.

Mackenzie had the 1st Natal Carbineers, 2nd Natal Carbineers, the Natal Mounted Rifles Brigade (Natal Mounted Rifles, Border Mounted Rifles, Umvoti Mounted Rifles, Zululand Mounted Rifles, Northern Districts Mounted Rifles), Transvaal Scottish (part), Pretoria Regiment, Natal Light Horse.

Entering Beersheba without opposition, he reached the railway on 24th April at Aritetis, a small station seventy miles north of Keetmanshoop and forty south of Gibeon. Mackenzie was now co-operating directly with the main movement of General Smuts from Keetmanshoop, and the retreating Germans were between the two forces. Van der Venter, pushing from the south, came into touch with the enemy at Kabus, and after an indecisive engagement, in which both sides lost prisoners, the Germans succeeded in reaching Gibeon, whence, as Mackenzie learned, they proposed to reach Windhoek by train. He sent out a small party to cut the line north of Gibeon, while the 9th Mounted Brigade went forward to engage the enemy.

At first the Germans were successful, but on 28th April our main force came up and inflicted on them a serious defeat. We took their

WHAT THE NATAL CARBINEERS LOOK LIKE AT GIBEON—SENTRY
OUTSIDE THE HOSPITAL.

two field guns, most of their transport, and some 200 prisoners, and released our own men who had fallen into their hands. We pursued them for twenty miles, and only the rocky and difficult country prevented their complete annihilation. We lost three officers and twenty men killed, among the former being Sir Thomas Watt's brother, Major J. H. Watt of the Natal Light Horse.

The circle of steel was now closing in upon Windhoek. By the 1st of May all the German colony south of Gibeon was in British hands, and Botha was threatening the capital from the west. On 10th May he was informed that Windhoek was prepared to surrender. With a small escort he reached the place, where he was met by the burgomaster, and terms of capitulation were arranged, and on the 12th at noon his army entered the town. In it were 3,000 Europeans and 12,000 natives. The German troops had withdrawn to Grootfontein, in the north-east of the colony, which, it was declared, was now the capital. The wireless station was found intact, and with its capture Germany had lost all her stations outside Europe.

After the entry of the troops under General Myburgh, a proclamation by General Botha was read in Dutch, English, and German, which placed the conquered territories under martial law, and drew attention to the futility of further resistance.

The capture of Windhoek meant virtually the possession of German South-West Africa, and the difficult operation had been carried through with the highest degree of skill and a minimum of loss. The enemy had been outnumbered, out-generalled, and, when necessary, out-fought, and by his leadership General Botha had performed a service, to use his former words, "of the utmost importance to the Empire and to South Africa." The British Prime Minister, in his speech at the Guildhall on 19th May, well described the difficulties of the campaign:

> Their undertaking has been no slight one. A force of about 30,000 men, rather over half of whom are mounted men, with guns, horses, medical stores, mules, and transports, have been conveyed oversea 500 and 700 miles, in addition to the large land force which has been operating on the German-Union frontier. All supplies, every pound of provisions for the men, much of the water for their consumption, every ton of forage for horses and mules, have had to be brought from Cape Town. All the railway material for rapid construction has also had to

GERMAN MOUNTED TROOPS

be brought from Cape Town, and all these men, horses, guns, supplies, and materials had to be landed at two ports, Luderitz and Walfisch, at which appliances for disembarkation for such operations had not been constructed. Then there was the sandy desert *veld*, eighty to a hundred miles wide, which had to be covered.

The real foe had not been the Germans, but the climate and the desert. Not even the dank forests of the Cameroons made a more uncomfortable fighting ground than those scorching wastes of Namaqualand, which were assuredly made for chameleons and salamanders, and not for man. A letter from a volunteer in General Botha's army gives a vivid picture of the hardships:

We have a far more difficult country to fight in, and a better equipped foe to fight against, than our soldiers had in the Boer War. Every day we have awful dust-storms lasting for hours and the shade temperature always over 100°. One day it was 113°. Still I'm ten times fitter than I ever was in my life, and have stuck all the marches in one heavy kit. Johannesburg has supplied 12,000 men for the front; that includes the Reef. Mounted men have a thin time. It is frightfully difficult getting enough water for ourselves let alone for animals.

We've struck a place far worse than Luderitzbucht for sand and wind; it blows like the devil from midday to dark, and all the tents are going to ribbons. Ours, which had been holding together in a miraculous manner for some days, went with a bang yesterday afternoon. The sand blows along just like sleet, and the wind has not even the advantage of being cool. We clean our shirts by spreading them in the sun three or four days. We have to raise little cairns of stones to mark where the shirts are, because they can be completely buried in a day. They have started dipping us just like sheep but we don't need prodding under with forked sticks as we go through the tank! I'm beginning to long for a holiday to get to some place where there's vegetable life and water.

A good many men have to be operated on to remove sand from their salivary glands, under their tongues. When they eat, the saliva, trying to force its way through, causes a good deal of pain and swelling. The sergeant of my section has just had three weeks in hospital from that cause. It's impossible even in a closed tent not to eat a good bit of sand when the wind is blowing. Two hundred Cape boys are employed day and night shovelling sand off 40 miles of railway. The train has a clear passage in the mornings, but returning in the evening finds as much as 4 feet of sand over the rails. Of course, we are allowed to wear goggles one would not wear them going into action but that is the only time that we should not.... I'm still keeping jolly fit, but I'll appreciate the Transvaal's vilest climate after this. Fighting men is a joke to fighting Nature.

One loss we have to record which cast a shadow over our success. Sir George Farrar, who had acted as Quartermaster-General to Sir Duncan Mackenzie's force, was killed in a railway accident near Gibeon on 18th May. He had played a great part in the modern history of South Africa. One of the old Uitlander chiefs, he had been condemned to death by President Kruger; he had fought gallantly in the South African War, and he had long been one of the leaders of the gold-mining industry. Toughly and compactly built, he was a born fighting man. In a world of smooth phrases, he spoke his mind bluntly and summarily, and his honesty of purpose and sincere, if undemonstrative, public spirit, were as unquestioned as his courage. His clear head and powers of organisation had been of inestimable use to General Botha in the campaign. The Empire was the poorer for the loss of a gallant and upstanding Englishman.

CHAPTER 4

The Campaign in the Cameroons

If during the summer the wheels of war dragged slowly in Western Europe, they moved with greater speed in those outland areas where the forces on both sides were small and the *terrains* vast and formidable. The summer saw the end of the South African campaign and a clear advance towards the subjugation of the Cameroons. Only in East Africa, where the British offensive was still in embryo, were the elements of decision still remote.

We left the Cameroons campaign in the early spring. By that time both of the railway lines running up from the coast were in our possession, and the enemy had been driven towards the interior plateau. Columns were entering the colony from north, east, and south, from Nigeria and the Chad territory and French Equatoria. The main forces of the enemy were believed to be on the head-waters of the Benue in the high country around Ngaundere. But there were other forces, notably one which operated near the coast just beyond the railheads of the two lines, and there were a number of fortified posts in the southern district towards the French Equatorian border.

Hence the campaign resolved itself into several distinct expeditions, directed to the "rounding up" of the various sections of the enemy. The railways had to be closely watched, for on them depended the existence of our central army. The rainy season soon began, and the dripping savannahs and the dank forests were as formidable a barrier as German machine guns.

In May the main Allied force under General Dobell was operating along the two railway lines. A French column under Colonel Mayer, starting from Edea, captured Eseka on 11th May, after some difficult forest fighting, where the Germans showed great skill in entrenching themselves at the river crossings.

CAMEROON ARTILLERY

A fortnight later, on 29th May, the same column had transferred itself to the northern railway, and driven the enemy from Njok to the north-west of that line. Late in the same month the southern columns fought actions at Monso and Besam, and on 25th June occupied the important post of Lome. The French had now taken practically all the country in the south up to their old boundary. The inhabitants seem to have risen against the Germans, and before the fall of Lome there had been a mutiny among the native troops. The torrential rains of July impeded further movements on this side, and the centre of interest shifted to the higher country towards the Nigerian border.

The first British incursions from Nigeria had been unhappily fated, our men with considerable losses having been driven from Garua and Nsanakong. In April the post of Gurin inside the Nigerian border was attacked by German troops from the Garua garrison. Gurin, a big rambling native town half a mile from the banks of the River Faro, was defended by Lieutenant Pawle of the Nigeria Regiment, a white sergeant, and forty native soldiers, and there was present also Mr. J. F. FitzPatrick, a political officer.

The German force consisted of sixteen Europeans, 350 native infantry, forty mounted infantry, and four Maxims. The British garrison occupied a small mud fort three-quarters of a mile from the town. Lieutenant Pawle was killed in the beginning of the fight, and, since the sergeant was soon severely wounded, the direction of the operations devolved upon Mr. FitzPatrick. The little fort held out for seven hours, and finally beat off the enemy. The German Maxims were in constant action, and fired some 60,000 rounds. A third of the native defenders were killed or wounded; the German losses were three Europeans and over thirty native soldiers killed, and a large number wounded.

The behaviour of the invaders was discreditable. In the town they murdered three elderly non-combatants, and stole everything portable, destroying what they could not remove. They carried off forty women, and hobbled one poor wretch and made him carry their ammunition across the fire zone. The German officers and the native soldiery they had trained were utterly regardless of the decencies of war. The defence of Gurin was a fine performance which deserves to be remembered. One pleasant incident may be recorded. Two native soldiers went off to Yola for help, and on their way met three Europeans.

These three had with them ten soldiers, and three carriers who

GERMAN AFRICAN TROOPS

had been soldiers in the dim and distant past. With this force, hearing that Gurin was being attacked by four hundred men, these three civilians set off to relieve the place, having armed the three ex-soldiers with a pickaxe apiece, being the deadliest thing available at that time and place. (For an account of the siege see *Blackwood's Magazine*. September 1915).

Next day the Yola column arrived at Gurin, having marched sixty-two miles in twenty-two hours. This column, under Colonel F. H. G. Cunliffe, composed of men of the West African Frontier Force, marched upon Garua, and prepared to reduce the position. It was assisted by a French column which had moved westward from the north-eastern border. On 11th June Garua surrendered unconditionally. (See appendix 1). This cleared the northern part of the colony except for one small German post which occupied a hill at Mora. The Allied columns then swept south, and on 29th June occupied Ngaundere, the most important German station in the Central Cameroons. The enemy retreated south-west towards Tibati, while the Allies followed, and on 11th June consolidated their position by taking the post of Tingr, 3,700 feet up on the plateau, and some seventy miles northwest of Ngaundere. The German forces had now been penned into the comparatively small area of hilly country between Tibati and the head-waters of the Sanaga River. On all four sides the Allied columns were closing in upon them.

The enemy had hoped for much from native support. But the Cameroon peoples seem to have welcomed the Allies, and the tribes on the Nigerian border were for the most part quiet. The Germans had promised the chiefs that they would be permitted to engage again in the slave trade, and this brought into the field a few of the half-conquered border clans. A column had to be dispatched to deal with these malcontents, and some notion of this lonely and dangerous task may be had from an officer's letter:—

The Ezzas are the most warlike tribe in these parts. We hear that they can mobilize 30,000 war boys. As I write, their camp, on the other side of the river from us, is alive with a couple of thousand Ezzas jumping about and howling. It is a cheery life with 2,000 of these beasts about 1,000 yards away! ...We heard they were to attack another part of the country, so we moved our camp on seven miles. The heat was tremendous, and both —— and —— were laid out with the sun. As our scouts told

CAMEROON DEFENSIVE POSITION

us the Ezzas were advancing, I had to go off with the police in the afternoon, the other men being in bed.

The Ezzas were coming to the attack by the way they had come four days previously; and as we marched along for the first two miles the stench was awful, dead bodies rotting in the sun. Every body had been decapitated. The Ezzas always take the head. A man is not a man till he can take a head home. After we had done two miles we came to the finish of the bush, and reached fine open country. There we tumbled on the Ezzas, a thousand strong. I had fifty police with me. The country the Ezzas were coming through was yam fields, our equivalent of ploughed fields, only the furrows are as high as your knee.

The Ezzas came on for us in fine style, taking cover. We put volley after volley into them, and when they got to within 200 yards they broke and ran. We followed at the double and drove them across the —— river. Just imagine five miles through ploughed fields at the double with a two-in-the-afternoon sun overhead. I was done to the world, but we found some cocoa-nuts, and the milk was very refreshing. We lost two killed and one wounded. The Isheri natives followed us, and every Ezza that fell lost his head. Of course, one can't stop this sort of thing; when natives see red it is red, and you can only thank God, it's not your head.

We next got a rumour that our camp was to be attacked, so we shifted another three miles on to high open country. No trees, so you can imagine what the heat is like with only a few palm leaves overhead. We had another go at the Ezzas the day before yesterday, and destroyed all their houses.

All this must sound rather tedious to you with the war at your doors, but it is very real to us, I can assure you, and one is just as dead and just as long dead from an African's bullet as from a German's. Also, there is no such thing as surrender at this game. It would be God help you if they got you.

East Africa

In the East African theatre, the reverse at Jassin in January was not retrieved during the summer by any conspicuous field success. On 29th April it was announced that Brigadier-General Tighe, a distinguished Indian officer, had been appointed to command the troops in British East Africa, with the rank of major-general. The main summer

The Summer Campaign in the Cameroons.

campaign was concerned with the shores of the Victoria Nyanza, and with the borders of Nyassaland and north-eastern Rhodesia. In April there were ineffective attempts to cut the Uganda railway, and there was a certain amount of fighting round the skirts of Kilimanjaro, but in general the high plateau showed little activity.

In March news came that a German column, under Captain Haxthausen, was marching to invade the Karungu district on the eastern shore of Lake Victoria. On the 9th a small force of King's African Rifles, under Lieutenant-Colonel Hickson, defeated the raiders on the Mara River, and scattered the column. All through May our patrols situated east of the lake between the German frontier and the Uganda railway were engaged in constant skirmishes. West of the lake our troops lay along the River Kagera, facing a German force which operated from the port of Bukoba. It was resolved to destroy the latter place in order to paralyze the enemy's operations in that district. The plan was to send an expedition by steamer from the British port at Kisumu on the eastern shore, about 240 miles away, and at the same time to advance our forces across the thirty miles which separated the Kagera River from Bukoba.

The expedition sailed on 20th June. It was under the command of Brigadier-General J. A. Stewart, and consisted of detachments of the King's African Rifles, the 1st Loyal North Lancashires, and the 25th Royal Fusiliers (the Legion of Frontiersmen), together with some artillery. Bukoba was reached on 25th June, when the enemy's forces, some 400 strong, were defeated after a sharp action, in which the Arab troops fought bravely on the German side. We captured most of their artillery, and inflicted heavy casualties. As a sidelight on German policy it may be noted that a Mohammedan standard of European manufacture was found in the house of the German *commandant*. This action kept the Uganda borders more or less quiet during the summer.

The shores of Lake Nyassa witnessed considerable naval activity. The German town of Sphinxhaven on the eastern shore was our chief objective, and on 3th May a naval force under Lieutenant Commander Dennistoun, supported by field artillery and a landing-party of King's African Rifles, attacked the place. After a bombardment from the water the enemy were driven out of the town, and a large number of rifles, ammunition, and military stores fell into our hands. It will be remembered that in August the British steamer *Gwendolen* had surprised and disabled the German armed steamer Von *Wissmann*, and driven her into the shelter of Sphinxhaven. The present attack meant the end of

Artllery firing

that unfortunate vessel, which was shelled and completely destroyed.

During the summer there was a good deal of guerilla warfare along the Nyassaland and north-eastern Rhodesian borders. The British forces were drawn from the Northern Rhodesia Rifles and the Northern Rhodesia Police. On 17th May there was a sharp action about twenty miles from the town of Fife, and on 28th June the Germans attacked in two bands on the Saisa River, near Abercorn. They were beaten off, but returned on 26th July, 2,000 strong, and besieged the place for six days before British reinforcements could arrive. In this section of the campaign we received invaluable support from Belgian troops, who defended the western shore of Lake Tanganyika and the frontier between that lake and Lake Mweru.

The early days of July saw the end of the German cruiser, the *Koenigsberg*. Ever since the close of October she had been sheltering some distance up the Rufiji River, in a place too shallow for the ordinary ship to approach. When we discovered her, we sank a collier at the mouth of the river, and so prevented her escape to open seas. Early in June Vice-Admiral King Hall, Commander-in-chief of the Cape station, brought out two river monitors, the *Severn* and the *Mersey*.

Our aircraft located the exact position of the *Koenigsberg*, which was surrounded by dense jungle and forest. On the morning of 4th July, the monitors entered the river and opened fire. The crew of the *Koenigsberg* had made their position a strong one by means of shore batteries which commanded the windings of the river, and look-out towers with wireless apparatus, which gave them the range of any vessel attacking. Owing to the thick jungle a direct sight of the enemy was impossible, and we had to work by indirect fire with aeroplanes spotting for the guns. The bombardment of 4th July, which lasted for six hours, set her on fire. The attack was resumed on 11th July, when the vessel was completely destroyed, either as a result of our shelling, or because she was blown up by her crew. The fate of this German cruiser, marooned for months far from the fresh seas among rotting swamps and jungles, is one of the most curious in the history of naval war.

Since the fighting during the summer was generally remote from the healthy uplands, and concerned with the low-lying Nyassaland and Uganda borders, the British troops suffered from other discomforts besides German guns. One officer' serving near the Victoria Nyanza, wrote:

If ever the Devil had a hand in the making of a country, this

GERMAN IRREGULARS

is the one he took most interest in, I fancy; while the country we are supposed to be trying to take is rather worse, if possible. To begin with, it's about the size of France, Germany, Switzerland, Belgium, and Holland in one. This puddle, one of many, is the size of Scotland, and one is frequently out of sight of land while steaming over it for hours at a time. Every known form of insect, and some peculiar to it alone, swarm on and round it. Tsetse fly and sleeping sickness, nine kinds of fever, each worse than the one before, revel in the district—in addition to hippo and crocs, which prevent bathing on the beaches.

But the life had its modest consolations:

In the intervals of shooting, or trying to shoot, Germans, I get a little game shooting—if possible, on their game preserves. Poaching, when one doesn't know if one is going to be poached oneself, is real sport.

German South-West Africa

The back of the resistance in German South-West Africa was broken when General Botha entered Windhoek on 12th May. The German troops had retired by the northern line towards Grootfontein, a position on which they could not hope to stand, and from which there was no obvious retreat. The war had now resolved itself into a "rounding-up" expedition, and some of the Union forces could be dispensed with. Accordingly, in May, General Smuts sent home a considerable part of his southern command. A few small actions were fought to the east of the capital by Colonel Mentz and General Manie Botha, when a considerable number of prisoners were taken with few British casualties.

Early in June the advance began up the northern line. The station of Omaruru was occupied, eighty miles from Windhoek, and a few days later General Botha was at Kalkfeld. The first objective was the junction of Otavifontein, where the northern railway forks, one branch going north to Tsumeb and the other northeast to Grootfontein. Against this position the Union forces advanced in three columns. To the left went General Manie Botha with the Mounted Free State Brigade. To the right General Lukin, who had originally commanded the column which Van der Venter had led north from the Orange River, marched with the 6th Mounted Brigade, composed of the South African Mounted Rifles. In the centre, along the railway line, moved General Botha and the Headquarters Staff. Otavifontein was taken on the morning of 2nd July, with few British casualties. The chief part was played by General Manie Botha, who in sixteen hours marched forty-two miles without a halt through the most difficult bush country. Lukin's flanking column covered forty-eight miles in twenty hours under the same conditions.

The fight at Otavifontein was the last serious German stand. The Union forces now moved towards Tsumeb, Colonel Myburgh on the right advancing between the two railway lines, and General Brits making a big westerly detour towards the great Etosha Pan. Brits's aim was to prevent the enemy retreating towards the Angola borders. His detour involved a march of 200 miles, and it effected its purpose. Meanwhile Myburgh's force, which was the operative part, moved laboriously over the sandy Waterberg plateau, where the mid-winter cold was bitter, and on 4th July came into contact with a force of 500 Germans at Gaub, about sixteen miles south of Tsumeb. The Germans made only a slight resistance, and left many prisoners in our hands.

The end was now in sight. Dr. Seitz, the German governor, opened communications with General Botha. At two o'clock on the morning of 9th July an unconditional surrender was agreed to. The German forces laid down their arms. The active troops were to be interned in such places as the Union Government should decide, the officers being allowed to retain their arms, and, on giving their parole, to reside where they pleased, and the other ranks retaining their rifles without ammunition.

The German police on duty at distant stations were to remain at their posts until relieved by Union troops. Civil officials in the employment of the German Government were to remain in their homes on parole. All other war material and all the property of the colony was placed at the disposal of the Union Government. General Lukin was entrusted with the details of the surrender, and the 6th Mounted Brigade and the 1st Infantry Brigade were left at Otavifontein to take charge of the prisoners and the war material.

General Botha could afford to be generous, for his conquest was complete. The numbers surrendering were officially reported as 204 officers and 3,293 of other ranks, while 37 field guns and 22 machine guns were captured. About 1,500 Germans were already prisoners in our hands. The total German casualties appear to have been between 300 and 400. Of the Union casualties in German territory we have as yet no official record; but the total casualties in the rebellion and the

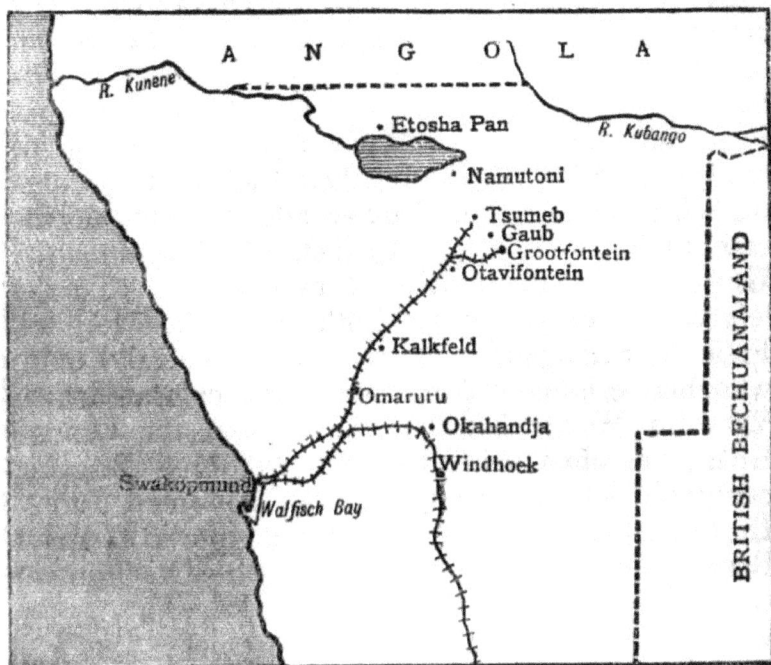

Map to illustrate the last stage of the
Damaraland Campaign.

Damaraland campaign seem to have been a little over 1,000.

Three hundred thousand square miles of territory had been conquered at a less cost than that of a minor action in the European theatre. British and Dutch had fought side by side with equal valour. The Boer commandos, with no particular uniforms and the loosest formation, showed all their old skill in desert campaigning. General Smuts's words were justified:

> Not only is this success a notable military achievement, and a remarkable triumph over very great physical climatic and geographical difficulties. It is more than that, in that it marks in a manner which history will record for all time the first achievement of the United South African nation, in which both races have combined all their best and most virile characteristics, and have lent themselves resolutely, often at the cost of much personal sacrifice, to overcome extraordinary difficulties and dangers in order to attain an important national object.

The King and the British Parliament telegraphed their congratulations to the South African leader, and his return to Cape Town was in the nature of a triumphant progress. In a speech which he made there on 24th July he revealed certain facts which showed the reality of the German menace to the integrity of the Union. A map was discovered in the enemy's hands showing the redistribution of the world after the "Peace of Rome, 1916." It placed the whole of Africa south of the Equator as part of the German Empire, with a small portion segregated as a Boer reserve. General Botha revealed the fact that as early as 1913 Maritz had been in treaty with Germany, and had inquired how far the independence of his proposed new republic would be guaranteed. The *Kaiser's* reply had been:

> I shall not only acknowledge the independence of South Africa, but even guarantee it, provided the rebellion starts immediately.

Well might General Botha observe that this guarantee painfully recalled the case of Belgium. He pointed out, too, that the German native policy constituted a danger to the whole sub-continent. The sufferings of the Hereros and other native tribes had left an ineradicable impression on his mind, and he told his hearers that the aborigines of Damaraland had regarded the coming of the British as a deliverance. In the Herero war the Germans, on their own admission, had killed 21,000 natives on the plea that they had massacred German women and children; but the records at Windhoek showed that only one child had perished. A Bastard chief who had refused to fight for the Germans in the recent campaign had had his family murdered in cold blood.

To estimate General Botha's services to the Empire we must keep in mind what might have happened had he behaved with less honour and loyalty. The rebellion, which enjoyed only a few weeks of life, might have grown to formidable dimensions and raged for years. Had he refrained from attacking the German colony a serious armed menace would have compelled the attention of Britain and distracted her efforts elsewhere. Had he conducted the campaign with less skill and less resolution it might have been long and costly, and would certainly have had a sinister effect on the political situation in the Union itself. His singlehearted devotion and brilliant generalship had saved his country from division, and had laid the foundations of a great and coherent South African nation.

CHAPTER 5

The Conquest of the Cameroons

We left the Cameroons campaign at the end of June 1915, when the French in the south had captured Lome, the Franco-British column in the north had taken Garua and Ngaundere, and the main force, moving up the midland railway, had reached Eseka and a position short of Wum Biagas, while the whole northern railway was in our hands. The Franco-British force had now grown to some 9,700, consisting of British, French, Belgian, and Indian native troops, trained and led by white officers and non-commissioned officers. The German strength was at the outset 3,000, including some 250 white officers, and though it was well munitioned, especially in the way of machine guns, the disparity of numbers suggested a short and simple campaign. But the Germans had potent allies in the country and the weather.

A territory half as large again as the German Empire in Europe had to be methodically "driven" so that no enemy resistance should anywhere remain, for it was impossible to bring matters to a decision by any one battle. It was a *terrain* created by nature for the defence. Food was abundant; there were few roads; the lines of communication for the attack stretched out alarmingly, and every fresh mile lessened their safety. Practically all supplies had to be transported by native carriers, whose loads were from 50 pounds to 60 pounds per man, and to defend the routes blockhouses had to be established every twenty miles whose garrisons greatly depleted the strength of the advancing columns.

The country everywhere was difficult to move in, and well-fitted for surprise attacks by the defence. In the coastal area there were dense dripping forests, choked with undergrowth, and seamed with broad and deep rivers. In the interior the *savannahs* were covered with elephant grass, sometimes twenty feet high, and broken up by rocky

British Infantry

heights whose boulder-strewn slopes were natural entrenchments and redoubts. The climate, too, especially in the coast districts and in the south, was hostile to rapid movement by white men. Tropical diseases, such as malaria, blackwater fever, and dysentery, waited to take toll of the overfatigued and the underfed.

Nevertheless, the Cameroons expedition was well within the experience of both France and Britain. It was the kind of campaign with which any Power with a long colonial record was familiar. The problems involved—leadership of native levies, improvisation under difficulties, swift marches through awkward country, the complex tropical transport—were those which Britain especially had faced for two hundred years. In the European theatre we were met by something new in our history, new indeed in the whole history of war.

Far other is this battle in the west
Whereto we move, there when we strove in youth
And brake the petty kings.

But in the Cameroons, we could apply a knowledge which our Allies had learned in Algiers and Tonkin, and we had acquired in a score of campaigns from Burma to Ashanti.

The Allied forces were under the command of Major-General Sir Charles Dobell, whose plan was a converging movement upon the German seat of government, which should in its progress sweep up the outlying centres of resistance. It was the same plan which had already been crowned with victory in German South-West Africa. The difficulties were indeed many. The enormous area and the lack of most modern forms of communication made accurate timing impossible, and left the details of each section of the fighting largely to the subordinate commanders.

After the occupation of Duala on September 27, 1914, the seat of the German Government was transferred to Yaunde, a station on the edge of the interior plateau, south of the Sanaga valley, and about 120 miles from the coast. Yaunde was obviously the proper object for the converging movement, and in March 1915 General Dobell arranged with General Aymerich, the officer commanding the French southern columns, for a general advance upon this point. The difficulties of the country held up the attack, and towards the end of June it became necessary to withdraw Colonel Mayer's French force, which had advanced to Eseka and beyond Wum Biagas, to the line of the Kele River. After this came the inevitable lull caused by the rainy season.

At the end of August, a conference took place at Duala between the Governor-General of French Equatoria, General Dobell, and General Aymerich, in which a plan for future operations was arrived at.

The different forces and their position at the moment may be briefly summarised. The main army under General Dobell was composed of two columns—the British, under Colonel Gorges, on the Sanaga River; and the French, under Colonel Mayer, farther south, on the Kele River. This represented the main thrust at Yaunde, and at the time was within fifty miles of the town. On the northern railway a British force under Lieutenant-Colonel Cotton was at Baré, and a detachment under Major Crookenden was at Ossidinghe, twenty miles from the Nigerian border. Farther north, Brigadier-General Cunliffe's force, which included the French column under Lieutenant-Colonel Brisset, which had marched from Lake Chad, was on the line Ngaundere-Kontcha-Gashaka, on the high ground above the upper streams of the Sanaga.

The country in its rear was not wholly cleared, for a strong body of the enemy was holding out in the Mountain of Mora, at the northern extremity of the Mandara range. In the south two main forces, under the direction of General Aymerich, had marched up the northern affluents of the Congo. On the east what the French called the Column of the Lobaye, under Lieutenant-Colonel Morisson, had moved west and north-west, taking Bania and Gaza; and another farther west, the Column of the Sangha, under Lieutenant-Colonel Hutin, had gone due north, taking Nola and Lome. The two forces had now joined hands, and were holding Dume and Bertua, about 130 miles east of Yaunde.

Finally, a detachment under Lieutenant-Colonel le Meillour was marching up the east side of the Spanish *enclave* of Rio Muni, to cross the Campo River and attack Ebolowa, which lay about sixty miles south by west of Yaunde. The German stronghold was therefore in the position of being ringed round on all sides. The enemy force nearest to its gates was General Dobell's main army; the farthest off was General Cunliffe's northern columns towards Ngaundere.

The real operations could not commence till early in October, but in the meantime General Cunliffe took advantage of the better weather in the north of the colony to make an attempt to reduce the mountain Mora, and so release the investing force for operations farther south. Mora, as he described it:

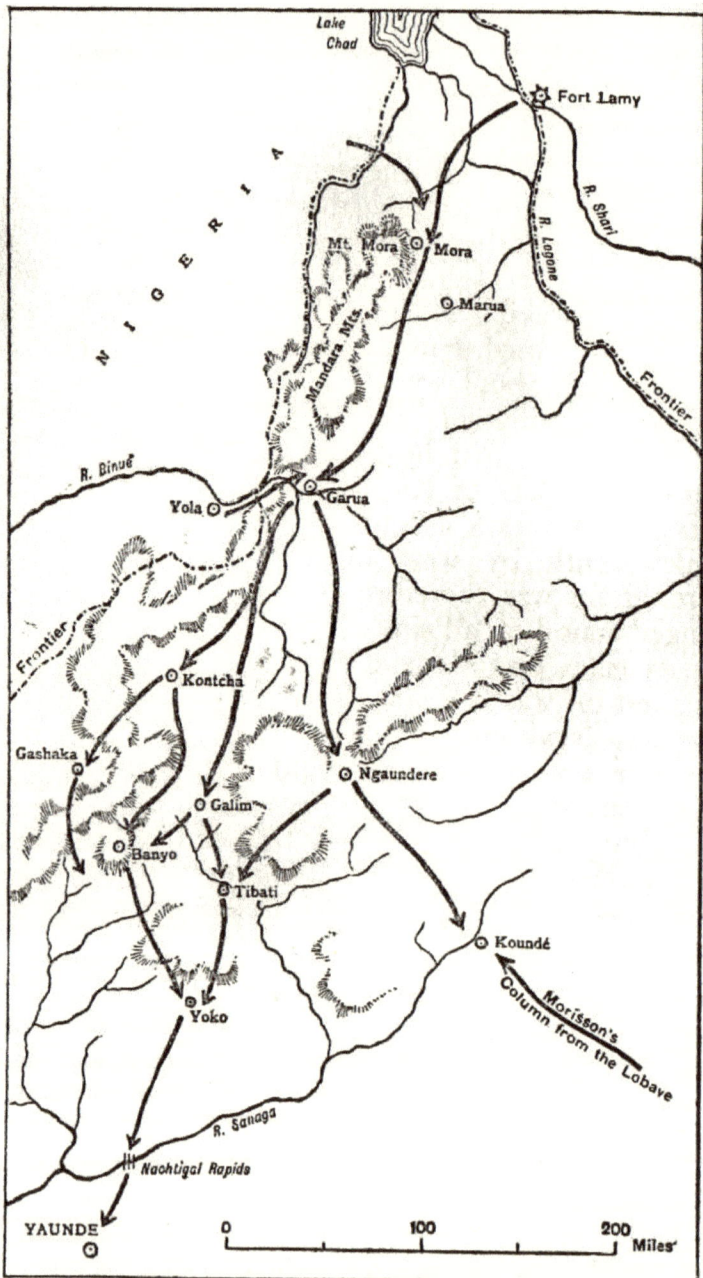

Operations of the Northern Forces under Cunliffe.

. . . . has a base perimeter of about thirty miles; it rises precipitously to a height of 1,700 feet, and its sides, which are so steep as to be accessible only in a few places to men using both hands and feet, are covered with huge boulders, affording excellent cover to the defenders.

He arrived four miles from the fort on 23rd August, and resolved to make the attack from Onatchke, a hill to the north, the summit of which was nearly level with Mora and separated from it by a deep valley 600 yards wide. From Onatchke three separate attacks were launched. In the third a part of the 1st Nigerian Regiment reached the summit, but were stopped by a redoubt, which they attempted with the bayonet, but failed to carry.

They remained in the position without food or water for forty-eight hours, till they were withdrawn. General Cunliffe decided that to take Mora he needed more artillery and more time, and as he was due to co-operate in the main advance he was compelled to relinquish the attempt for the present, and leave troops behind to invest it.

The main movement against Yaunde began on the 9th of October, when the Nigeria and Gold Coast troops of Colonel Gorges' column captured Wum Biagas. Meanwhile Colonel Mayer, advancing from the Kele River, occupied Sende on 25th October, and Eseka five days later. There was a short lull which was occupied in improving the routes. The bush track from Edea to Wum Biagas was converted into a good motor road, and railway communications with Eseka were all but completed. Where the country did not permit of motor or rail traffic, a force of 7,000 carriers was employed.

The next advance was on a wide front. Colonel Gorges aiming at the point Dschang Mangas, and Colonel Mayer at the road which connected Yaunde with the coast village of Kribi. The forest part of the advance was hotly contested; but by the beginning of the third week of December Colonel Gorges had reached open country, and on the 17th Dschang Mangas was taken. Colonel Mayer had an ordeal no less severe; but after five days' fighting he took Mangeles on 21st December. Meanwhile the British column had pushed on, finding the resistance of the enemy everywhere slackening, and on the first day of 1916 it entered Yaunde.

In the north there had been some spirited campaigning. General Cunliffe directed Colonel Brisset's French column to move on Tibati, Lieutenant-Colonel Webb-Bowen's column on Galim, and Ma-

12-LB GUN AT DSCHANG

jor Crookenden's force from Ossidinghe on Bamenda. Meanwhile Lieutenant-Colonel Cotton moved from Baré against Dschang. General Cunliffe's main body advanced from Kontcha against the mountain Banyo, which was one of the strongest German positions in the colony. On 22nd October Crookenden reached Bamenda, and on 6th November Cotton took Dschang. The two forces then moved on Fumban, which they took on 2nd December with the assistance of a detachment of General Cuncliffe's troops. Cunliffe himself had been engaged in the reduction of Banyo Mountain, a stronghold of the type of Mora, and succeeded at daybreak on the 6th of November after an action which, in the words of his report:

> May be justly described as one of the most arduous ever fought by African troops.

A letter from an officer serving in the force is worth quotation as a description of a very fine feat of arms:—

> From Banyo the enemy's position on the mountain looked grim and stupendous, huge rocky boulders standing out prominently right up to the very top, and the sides of the mountain bristling with strongly built *sangars*. We began our attack early on the morning of 4th November. The infantry, advancing from different directions, covered by the fire from our three guns, worked their way up slowly and doggedly foot by foot, climbing over rocks and tearing their way through the thorny scrub and long grass, under a heavy rifle and Maxim-gun fire from the enemy's *sangars* (breastworks), and concealed snipers among the rocks. By the evening most of the companies had managed to struggle halfway up the hill, there getting what shelter they could from the incessant fire of the enemy aided by the light of fireballs and rockets. Officers and men, exhausted and drenched with rain, hung on determinedly to the ground gained.
>
> At dawn on the morning of the 5th they started climbing once more. Our troops having got directly under the first line of *sangars*, the enemy, in addition to rifle and Maxim-gun fire, started rolling down rocks and throwing dynamite bombs. All that day our men gradually worked their way up, capturing a small stone redoubt and *sangar* here and there. Owing to the paucity of gun ammunition, the covering artillery fire could not afford the infantry the essential assistance so imperatively necessary on these occasions.

BRITISH MACHINE-GUN POSITION

Fortunately, a convoy arrived on the afternoon of the 5th bringing with it two hundred more rounds of gun ammunition, which, hurriedly sent out, enabled the guns to fire somewhat more rapidly till the upward advance of the infantry and their proximity to the summit rendered it too dangerous to continue their fire.

Darkness set in early that evening—at 5 p.m. Heavy clouds rolled up from the west, and an hour or two later a terrific thunderstorm burst over the mountain. Heavy firing and the explosion of bombs and fireballs still continued. There seemed reason to fear that owing to the exhaustion of our men from want of sleep and violent physical exhaustion they would never succeed.

A misty morning prevented our seeing what was happening as dawn broke on the morning of the 6th, but as only intermittent firing was going on success seemed assured, and sure enough as the mist dispersed a white flag could be seen on the top of the hill and our men silhouetted against the skyline.

The enemy completely demoralised by the determined advance of our men despite heavy losses, had during the night of the 5th-6th broken up into small scattered parties and fled in several directions. Owing to the darkness of the night, the noise of rain and thunder, and their knowledge of the intricate nature of the country, the majority of the enemy parties had managed to worm their way down the hill without being intercepted by our infantry, only, however, to run up against the detached posts of our mounted infantry who were guarding all roads in the vicinity. These enemy parties then fired a few wild shots and scattered into the long grass which covers the whole country, and where it is difficult to follow up and capture them.

On the top of the mountain an extraordinary sight presented itself. Scattered in all directions were broken furniture, burst-open trunks and tin boxes, blankets, bedding, clothes, tins of food, broken bottles of wine and beer, smashed-up rifles, gramophones, telephones, and a medley of every conceivable sort of thing. There were two fine cement-built reservoirs of water, a vegetable garden, caves converted into granaries and filled with mealies and guinea corn, cattle, pigs, and sheep browsing about, and chickens galore.

This was very clear and conclusive proof of the conviction of

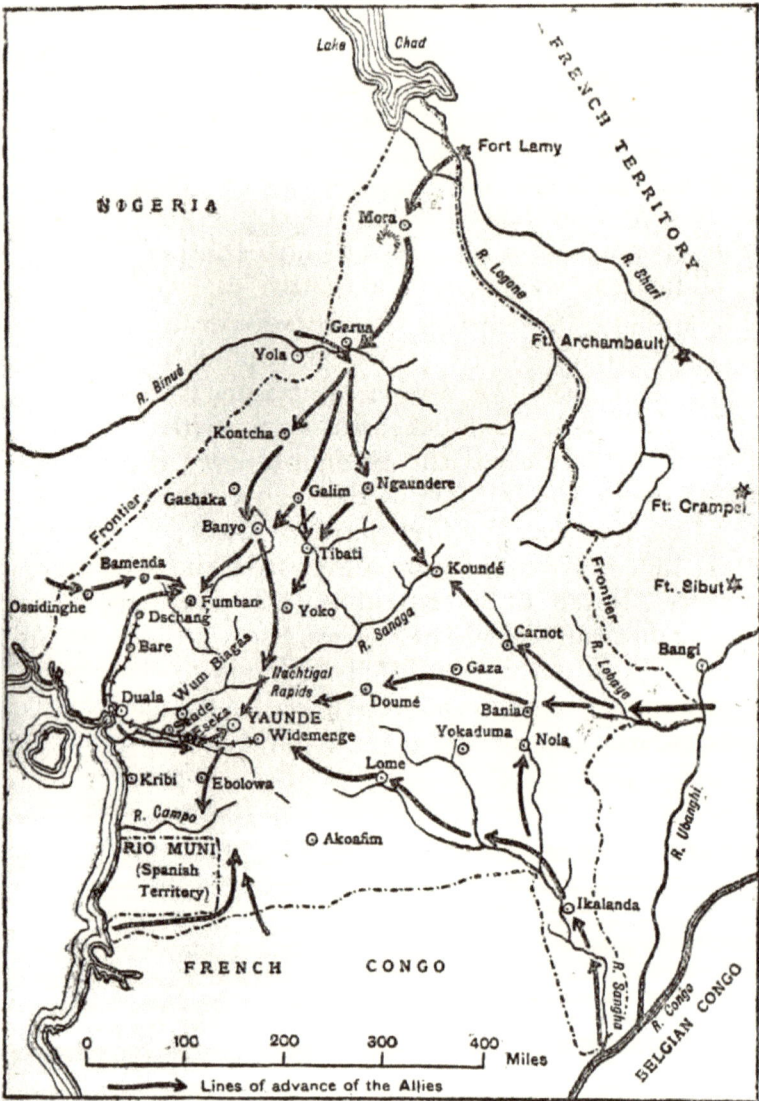

The Conquest of the Cameroons.

the Germans that the mountain was impregnable, and that they meant to hold it indefinitely and continually worry us.

During the action at Banyo the two columns of Colonel Brisset and Colonel Webb-Bowen had entered Tibati. General Cunliffe's forces were now converging on the Sanaga River by way of Yoko, which was entered by Brisset on 1st December. On January 4, 1916, the crossing of the Sanaga was seized at the Nachtigal Rapids, a point only forty miles north of Yaunde, and connection was established with General Aymerich on the east. Brisset and Webb-Bowen entered the German capital immediately after General Aymerich, and only a few days after the place had fallen to Gorges.

Such precision in concentration would have been admirable in any campaign; it was especially admirable in one involving such vast distances and precarious communication. General Dobell wrote in his dispatch:

> It is, I think, a remarkable feat, that troops that had fought and marched for a period of seventeen months should have converged on their objective within a few days of one another. (See Appendix 2).

The rest was merely a matter of sweeping up. The bulk of the German troops not already prisoners fled south-westward towards Spanish territory. Ebolowa was occupied on 19th January, and Colonel Morisson with a strong French force chased the remnants over the Campo River inside the borders of Spanish Guinea. Among the fugitives was the German Governor, Ebermaier, and the German commander-in-chief, Zimmermann. There only remained the mountain Mora in the far north, where the garrison still held out.

Generous terms were offered—officers to be allowed to retain their swords, native ranks to be released and given free passage to their homes, all Europeans to go to England as prisoners of war—and on 18th February Captain von Raben, the *commandant*, surrendered. There were now no Germans left in the Cameroons, and the conquest of the country was completed.

Had the Cameroons campaign been the only hostilities in which Britain at the time was engaged, its happy issue would have been a cause of pride to the whole Empire, and would have brought great honour to the men who contrived it. It was economical, well-conceived, and admirably executed. Few tropical wars have involved more intricate problems of transport or more toilsome marches. Take the case of General Cunliffe's northern force. When it entered Yaunde in January it had marched and fought continuously over 600 miles since the 18th of September, and its line of communication with the base at Ibi was 400 miles long.

The campaign revealed the fine fighting qualities of the West African native troops, both French and British; General Dobell paid tribute to the bravery and unshaken cheerfulness of the Senegalese, and the Nigerians of the West African Frontier force, to whom "no day appears to be too long, no task too difficult." General Cunliffe's testimony is worth quoting:—

> This report would be incomplete were I to conclude it without a word of praise to the native rank and file of the Nigerian Regiment, who have borne the brunt of the fighting, as well as to those natives, the transport carriers, who have toiled incessantly under heavy loads, and at times also under heavy fire, to keep the troops in the field supplied with food and munitions. The Nigerian Regiment is composed of men of many different tribes—their characteristics, traditions, and even their language differ as widely as does the food to which they are accustomed. They have been called upon to take part in a great struggle, the rights and wrongs of which they can scarcely have been expected dimly to perceive. They have been through the, to them, extremely novel experience of facing an enemy armed with modern weapons and led by highly-trained officers. Their rations have been scanty, their barefoot marches long and trying, and their fighting at times extremely arduous, yet they have not been found wanting either in discipline, devotion to their officers, or personal courage.

In the case of such troops everything depended upon the leading. They were like great schoolboys, and, if properly handled, would go anywhere and do anything. The campaign proved that France and Britain had not lost the art of providing the type of regimental officer who by his tact and courage can win and retain the affection of tribesmen.

German Colonisation.

The German garrison of the Cameroons—as was clear from captured documents—had confidently believed that they could hold out till the end of the European struggle. Their hopes were disappointed. Germany's grandiose African enterprises had by the middle of February 1916 been reduced to the single colony of East Africa, where General Smuts's columns were already pressing in upon the interior railways. If such far-away happenings seemed trivial compared to the desperate contest on the main battle-ground, the conquest of the German colonies had none the less a vital bearing upon the policy of the war. In striking at German Africa the Allies were not attacking irrelevant and half-forgotten dependencies, but an integral part of the German scheme of world-empire.

In an earlier chapter we have seen why Germany first came to Africa, and how she won her footing. German colonisation was a reasoned policy, not the haphazard work of individuals which gradually grows into a national purpose; and, like all reasoned policies, in its first stages it marched fast. She had a clear aim—to provide producing grounds for raw material, military outposts, and observation stations.

Such an aim, be it said, was not colonisation, which is more than a chain of plantations, and much more than a string of garrisons. Colonisation involves *settlement*—the adoption of emigrants of the new land as their home, the administration of that new land with a view to its own future, and not with regard merely to the ambitions of the parent country.

Mere exploitation is not colonisation, as the Dutch and the Portuguese found. The inhabitants must get their roots down, must acquire a local patriotism as well as a patriotism of origin. The duty to the land itself must be recognised, and not less the duty to the older masters who continue to live side by side with the new. A true colony is a slow business, an organic growth rather than a mechanical construction, and true colonies the German possessions had never been, for the root of the matter was neglected.

Further, the German colonies, being what they were, were a constant menace to their neighbours. If one man is digging trenches to drain his farm, and another digs to make the foundations of a fort, there is nothing in common between the two, and no possibility of harmonious neighbourship. The German colonies were part of the Pan-Germanist propaganda, like the Bagdad railway or the fortress of Tsing-tau. They represented one side of the plan of expansion, as the control of Mesopotamia represented the other. There was this difference between the two sides, that while the extension south-eastward of the Central European Powers might be possible by military strength only, the maintenance of armed colonies demanded a navy.

Again, and again the enthusiasts of the German Navy League used the colonial argument to support their pleas; Germany in her striving after *Weltmacht* must have her oversea garrisons, and an omnipotent navy was needed as a link between them. Given that navy, their strategic value would have been great. German East Africa was on the southern flank of the road to India, as Mesopotamia was on the northern. With German influence on both sides of the great waterway to the East, the most vital interests of Britain would have been menaced. The *Drang nach Osten* was largely and subtly conceived.

Shortly after the fall of the Cameroons Professor Ernst Haeckel added to the gaiety of nations by discoursing in an American magazine on Germany's future plans. The world had not hitherto associated Professor Haeckel with high politics; but in these bad times all the *gelehrten* were mobilised, and the venerable author of *Welträthsel* with the rest. He explained that Germany needed an empire, not like England from lust of gold, or like France for vain glory, or like Italy from megalomania, or like Russia because of sheer barbarous greed, but because she was overcrowded at home, and wanted a dumping-ground for her surplus population.

Africa was to be a substantial part of that empire; the Congo especially, which would come to Germany as a consequence of the espousal of Belgium. The whole of Central Africa from sea to sea would be German, while the Cape would be restored to Holland, and Egypt to the Turks, and perfidious Britain would depart from the continent altogether.

The plea for settlement was out of date, for Germany in recent years had shown no desire for settlers, and the tide of her emigration had long ago ebbed. Professor Haeckel's dream could only come true if the Allies were beaten to the ground. The doom of the German colonies was sounded with the first gun that roared on the Belgian border. Their continuance was forbidden by every consideration of strategy and common sense, by the Allies' knowledge of what Germany aimed at, of the purpose which she had destined her colonies to serve. She had never shown the true colonising spirit.

As there is an honourable *camaraderie* among pioneers in wild countries, so there is a certain freemasonry among those Powers which have experimented in colonisation. Their object is to make a garden of the desert, to create a new land which, while owing allegiance to the motherland, shall yet be free to follow its own natural development, and shall be administered for its own advantage. If a tropical country, it owes duties to the soil and the former inhabitants; if a white man's land, it seeks settlement and the advent of a new nation. But a colony which is used as an armed post and a point of vantage in some great strategical game is outside this comity. It is eternally a spy, an alien, and a potential disturber of the peace. During its life it will be regarded with just suspicion, and its end will be unlamented.

CHAPTER 6

The Conquest of East Africa

The close of 1917 saw what had once been the colony of German East Africa wholly in British hands, though fighting still continued inside the marches of Mozambique. The story of the campaign which produced this result deserves to be studied in the closest detail, both for its masterly strategy, its picturesque interest, and its superb record of human endurance. In a work such as this it can be treated only on broad lines, for it was no more than an episode in the great struggle of the nations. But even the barest sketch will reveal the extraordinary difficulties of the campaigning and the magnitude of the performance alike of conquerors and conquered.

In the early days of 1915, when the slender British forces were definitely on the defensive. The Germans in East Africa were like the Germans in Europe, with enemies on all sides and blockaded by sea; but the enemies were little more than a handful, and the encirclement was futile. Operating on interior lines, and with communications immensely superior to those of his opponents, the problem of von Lettow-Vorbeck was at the start an easy one. The main British forces had been drawn chiefly from India. There were one regular British infantry battalion—the Loyal North Lancashires—a number of battalions of the King's African Rifles, contingents from South Africa, and various irregular units, mounted and unmounted, raised among the settlers. The little army was starved of men, for it was the British policy that, as far as possible, no troops should be used in East Africa which could be employed in the main theatre in Europe.

In November 1914, as we have seen, General Aitken had failed signally at Tanga. In January 1915 came a second British defeat at Jassin. In April of that year Major-General Tighe became Commander-in-Chief, but he had not the strength to begin serious offensive op-

1st King's African Rifles

erations. During 1915 there were a number of minor engagements, chiefly on the Uganda side and in the south-west, where a small force was at work on the Rhodesia frontier, while Belgian troops were also busy on the Congo border. But at the beginning of 1916 the honours lay clearly with the Germans. They had their colony intact, as Governor von Schnee proudly proclaimed; and they believed that, since they were self-supporting, they could resist any reinforcements which the British could bring. Tropical Africa was their main defence; climate and distance, swamps and mountains, were better safeguards than numbers and munitions. And they had cause for their confidence, for they had boldly kept the initiative. They were for ever raiding the Uganda and the Voi-Maktau railways, and in the gap of Kilimanjaro, the main gate of the north, they held Taveta and the line of the Lumi River inside British territory.

In considering the remarkable achievements of General Smuts and his South African contingents, we must not forget the long, heartbreaking struggle of the troops, white and coloured, who held the fort till February 1916. For eighteen months they had borne the heat and burden of the climate, without chance of leave, without adequate supplies, with little to cheer them in their past record, and with no hope of an offensive in the future. One white officer, often in the early twenties, with a handful of natives was left to patrol a long length of line in the face of vigilant and aggressive enemies. In that wide and solitary land there was none of the stimulus which comes from a consciousness of supports at call and neighbours near.

The time was soon to come when the little army was caught up in a great movement, and swept the enemy's domain from all points of the compass. But let us recognise the desperate strain on mind and body of the far-flung lines of defence which during 1915 sat in dreary and perilous vigil on the northern borders.

At the beginning of 1916 East Africa was the only colony left to Germany. She had lost successively Togoland, South-West Africa, and the Cameroons, and she was the more determined to cling to her richest possession. She hoped by her victories over the Allies in Europe to be able to dictate terms as to Africa, and her terms were not less than a German domination from the Atlantic to the Indian Ocean, embracing British and German East Africa, the Belgian and French Congo, Angola, the Cameroons, Nigeria, and all West Africa to Cape Verde. Mittel-Afrika had taken as definite a shape as Mittel-Europa. She wished it strategically as a flank guard for her conquests in

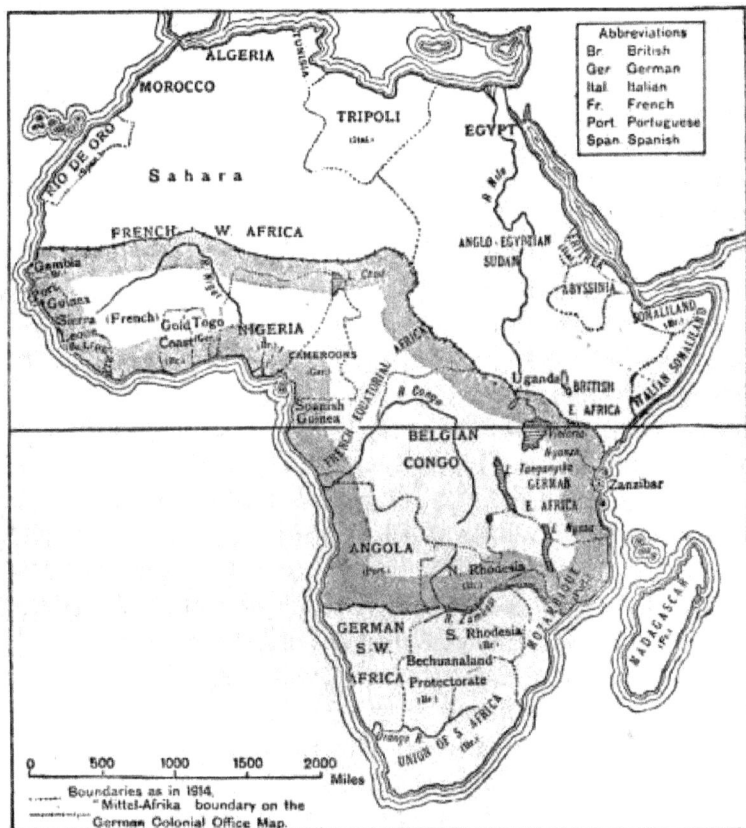

Africa, showing (by the shaded boundary) the region included in the German Colonial Office Map of Mittel-Afrika (Berlin, 1917).

the Near East; she wished it as a controlled producing ground of those raw materials which were disturbing the minds of her economists; she wished it as a recruiting ground for an army of a million men, trained in the German fashion, which would terrorise the unwarlike peoples of the few African territories that remained to other Powers.

Herr Emil Zimmermann dreamed of a day when Mittel-Afrika would have a population of fifty million natives and half a million Germans; when great cities would have sprung up on Chad and Tanganyika and the Congo; and when the Lake Chad express, carrying a freight of German bagmen, would run regularly from Berlin. The Emperor had ordered his people in Africa to hold out to the last; and, with such a dream before them, it was their business to yield nothing till the final victory in Europe should gain everything.

★★★★★★

The German views on Africa will be found set out in General Smuts's address to the Royal Geographical Society (*Geographical Journal*, March 1918); in Emil Zimmermann's *Das Deutsche Kaisserrich Mittel-Afrika als Grundlage einer neuen Deutschen Weltpolitik* (1917), translated into English by Edwyn Bevan, 1918; in Dr. Solf's article in the *Colonial Calendar* for 1917, and in his numerous speeches; and in the article by Delbrück in the *Preussische Jahrbucher* for February 1917.

★★★★★★

The German general, von Lettow-Vorbeck, was an officer of the General Staff, who had once been Chief of Staff in the Posen district. He came to Africa in the spring of 1914, and set himself at once to develop the local levies. For his native troops he drew upon the best fighting races of Africa—Sudanese, Somalis, Zulus, and Wanyamwezi. He was a specialist in machine guns, and he saw the advantage of that weapon for bush fighting. His men were immune against tropical diseases; they knew the tangled country like their own hand; and his transport, being entirely by porters, was not incommoded by the bad roads.

Moreover, like most of his countrymen, he had no conscience as to the treatment of natives, and could enforce discipline by the lash and the chain. His chief difficulty was likely to be shortage of arms and ammunition, for the large stock with which he began the war was bound to be depleted. He was fortunate, however, in receiving various unexpected windfalls. When the *Koenigsberg* was destroyed by our warships in the Rufiji River in July 1915, her guns were saved and

GENERAL PAUL EMIL VON LETTOW-VORBECK

moved up country. We proclaimed a blockade of the coast on February 28, 1915; but three ships managed to get through—the *Adjutant* to Dar-es-Salaam in February 1915, the *Rubens* from Hamburg to Mansa Bay in April 1915, and the *Maria* to Sudi Bay in March 1916.

Ammunition was also manufactured in local workshops, as were other supplies—such as benzine, paraffin, leather, rubber, and quinine. All the resources of a rich colony were adapted to the business of war. It is difficult to overpraise the vigour and adaptability of the German effort, and in von Lettow the colony had a commander of infinite resource, courage, and persistence. Before the arrival of General Smuts, he disposed in the field of a force larger and better equipped than the thin lines of the besiegers; and even after the arrival of the South African contingents he had an army scarcely inferior to ours in effectives, better adapted for tropical warfare, and with a far simpler problem before it.

It was the first time in history that a British Army had in a tropical wilderness encountered an enemy force officered by highly-trained Europeans. The combination meant that every advantage of terrain and climate would be most cunningly used against us. Since our aim was to conquer the country and expel the enemy or compel him to surrender, our offensive involved interminable marches in areas most unsuitable for a force with wheeled transport moving far from its base. In extent the colony was as large as Germany, Italy, Switzerland, Holland, and Denmark taken together. The coast line on the Indian Ocean was 470 miles long, the western frontier from Lake Victoria to Lake Nyasa some 700 miles, and from Dar-es-Salaam on the east to the terminus of the Central Railway at Tanganyika on the west the distance was 787 miles.

The land rose in tiers from the eastern coastal plain to a plateau which broke down steeply towards the trough of the Central Lakes. In the north the frontier with British East Africa was for the most part a chain of mountains, the Usambara and Pare ranges culminating in the great massif of Kilimanjaro. The western border, between the lakes, was also mountainous; so difficult that the Belgian force could not invade enemy territory direct from the Congo, but had to be moved north-east round the volcanic ranges to Uganda before they could find a starting-point. In the south-west a mountain range closed the gap between Lakes Tanganyika and Nyasa, and blocked the advance from North-Eastern Rhodesia. More notable still, a chain of ranges—the Nguru, Uluguru, and Mtumba mountains—lay from north to

East African Mounted Rifles

south on the edge of the plateau and the coastal plain, and so formed a series of rallying points for the enemy's defence. Two railways ran from east to west—those from Tanga to Moschi, and from Dar-es-Salaam to Tanganyika. We had but one sea base—Mombasa—and everything for the critical northern front had to be landed there.

The struggle, wrote General Smuts, was largely:

A campaign against Nature, in which climate, geography, and disease fought more effectively against us than the well-trained forces of the enemy.

Of the nature of the campaign he has also written:—

It is impossible for those unacquainted with German East Africa to realise the physical, transport, and supply difficulties of the advance over this magnificent country of unrivalled scenery and fertility, consisting of great mountain systems alternating with huge plains; with a great rainfall and wide unbridged rivers in the regions of all the mountains, and insufficient surface water on the plains for the needs of an army; with magnificent bush and primeval forest everywhere, pathless, trackless, except for the spoor of the elephant or the narrow footpath of the natives; the malarial mosquito everywhere except on the highest plateaux; everywhere belts infested with the deadly tsetse fly, which makes an end of all animal transport; the ground almost everywhere a rich black or red cotton soil, which any transport converts into mud in the rain or dust in the drought.

In the rainy seasons, which occupy about half the year, much of the country becomes a swamp, and military movements become impracticable. And everywhere the fierce heat of equatorial Africa, accompanied by a wild luxuriance of parasitic life, breeding tropical diseases in the unacclimatised whites. These conditions make life for the white man in that country far from a pleasure trip: if, in addition, he has to make long marches on short rations, the trial becomes very severe; if, above all, huge masses of men and material have to be moved over hundreds of miles in a great military expedition against a mobile and alert foe, the strain becomes unendurable.

And the chapter of accidents in this region of the unknown! Unseasonable rains cut off expeditions for weeks from their supply bases; animals died by the thousand after passing through an unknown fly belt; mechanical transport got bogged in the

German Colonial troops at Kilimanjaro

marshes, held up by bridges washed away or mountain passes demolished by sudden floods. And the gallant boys marching far ahead under the pitiless African sun, with the fever raging in their blood, pressed ever on after the retreating enemy, often on much-reduced rations and without any of the small comforts which in this region are real necessities. In the story of human endurance, the campaign deserves a very special place; and the heroes who went through it uncomplainingly, doggedly, are entitled to all recognition and reverence. Their Commander-in-Chief will remain eternally proud of them.

In the autumn of 1915 Sir Horace Smith-Dorrien, the former commander of the British Second Army in Flanders, had been appointed Commander-in-Chief of the forces in East Africa. Accompanied by a large staff, he sailed for the Cape; but there, persistent ill-health compelled him to return to England. At the beginning of 1916 General Smuts was appointed in his place, and on 19th February he arrived at Mombasa. As we have seen earlier, General Smuts had conducted brilliantly the southern operations in the German South-West African campaign, and he had since held the portfolio of Defence in the Union Government. In the South African War of 1899-1902 he had been one of the most mobile and successful of the Boer generals. As he put it whimsically:

> I believe it is generally admitted that in the Boer War I covered more country than any other commander in the field on either side—and my movement was not always in the direction of the enemy!

He had now to face the reverse problem—how to bring to book an evasive and swiftly-moving enemy in a country compared with which the High Veld was a parterre.

Large contingents had been raised in South Africa, some of which had already arrived on the battleground. There were two formed divisions in the country, apart from the troops on the lakes and the Rhodesia and Nyasaland forces—the 1st Division, under General Stewart, at Longido; and the 2nd Division, under General Tighe, on the Voi-Maktau line. The enemy strength was estimated at 16,000 men, of whom 2,000 were white—a number slightly less than the army which General Smuts now commanded—and its main force was concentrated in the Kilimanjaro region to bar the gates of the north. But since von Lettow had behind him the Tanga Railway and the good

The British advance on Kilimanjaro

roads connecting it with the Central Railway, he was in a position to move troops with speed to the coastal plain, should a landing be threatened there.

General Smuts's first task was to decide upon a plan of campaign. Since Britain controlled the sea, it seemed the natural course to force a landing at Tanga and Dar-es-Salaam, and move into the interior along the railway lines. Such a course would give us at once much shorter communications with our bases at Durban and Cape Town, and would enable us to advance to the tableland by the valleys of the many east-flowing rivers. This was undoubtedly the plan which the enemy expected us to adopt, but he had to reckon with a master of the unexpected.

General Smuts decided to "drive" the country from north to south, while his subsidiary forces, British and Belgian, moved eastward from Lake Victoria, from Lake Kivu, from Tanganyika and Nyasa. It was a plan which at first sight seemed to verge on the impossible. In moving south, he had to force the gap of Kilimanjaro, where the Germans were strongly entrenched; he had to cross many rivers and lateral valleys; he had to face three knots of difficult mountain-land; above all, till he won the Tanga Railway, he must have one single precarious line of communication through Voi and Maktau. More: even with the Tanga Railway, even with the Central Railway in his hands, his position would not be easy, for the enemy might be expected so to destroy these lines that they would take months to repair. Indeed, he could look for no certain additional communications till he found them by water on the Rufiji.

But General Smuts had good reason for his decision. His main forces were massed on the northern front, and there was no time before the rains came to alter General Tighe's dispositions. He knew, too, the deadly climate, and he did not wish to subject his men to the fevers of the coastal plain with the rains due in a month's time. So far as possible he hoped to fight on the high lands, or at any rate to have uplands adjacent for rest camps and hospitals. Again, he wished to split the enemy country, as Sherman split the Confederacy by his march through Georgia. If his main force took the central road from north to south, and subsidiary armies pressed in from the west, and in due course detachments landed on the coast and pushed westward, the enemy would be caught, not between two but between a multitude of fires.

He knew the difficulty of rounding up a mobile force and clearing a savage country, and he was well aware that it could not be achieved by a stately progress against a fully warned enemy. He wanted a surprise, a series of surprises, for no Fabian strategy could effect his purpose. Therefore, he adopted a plan which von Lettow had not dreamed of, and flung himself into the wilds, trusting to good fortune to pick up new communications as he proceeded. It was a plan only possible for a commander who had implicit faith in himself and in his men. He wrote:

> I am sure, it was not possible to conduct the campaign successfully in any other way. Hesitation to take risks, slower moves, closer inspection of the auspices, would only have meant the same disappearance of my men from fever and other tropical diseases, without any corresponding compensation to show in the defeat of the enemy and the occupation of his country.

The first step was to force the passage between the flanks of Kilimanjaro and the Pare mountains. Before his arrival General Tighe had done good work in the way of preparation. The 1st Division had occupied Longido and linked it up with the railhead at Lake Magadi, and the 2nd Division had taken Serengeti. The railway from Voi was slowly creeping forward from Maktau. After a careful reconnaissance General Smuts resolved to attack at once, in order to achieve his purpose before the heavy rains began in the end of March. Across the mouth of the gap, between Kilimanjaro and the Pare Mountains, ran the River Lumi, joining the Ruwu, which flowed from Lake Jipe along the northern base of the Pare.

On this line the enemy held an apparently impregnable position. Clearly there was no way of turning it on the south, for the Pare cliffs rose sheer from the river. General Smuts's plan was to direct the 1st Division, under General Stewart, from Longido across thirty-five miles of waterless bush to the gap between Meru and Kilimanjaro, and thence to the place called Somali Hauser, west of Moschi. They were then to move south-east to Kahe, on the Tanga Railway, in the hope of cutting off the retreat of the enemy in the gap. The 2nd Division, under General Tighe, was to attack in front towards Taveta, assisted on the right by the 1st South African Mounted Brigade, under General Van Deventer.

The 1st Division started at dusk on 5th March, Van Deventer moved out by night on the 7th, and the 2nd Division advanced at dawn on the 8th. After a sharp fight at Salaita hill, the Lumi was crossed and

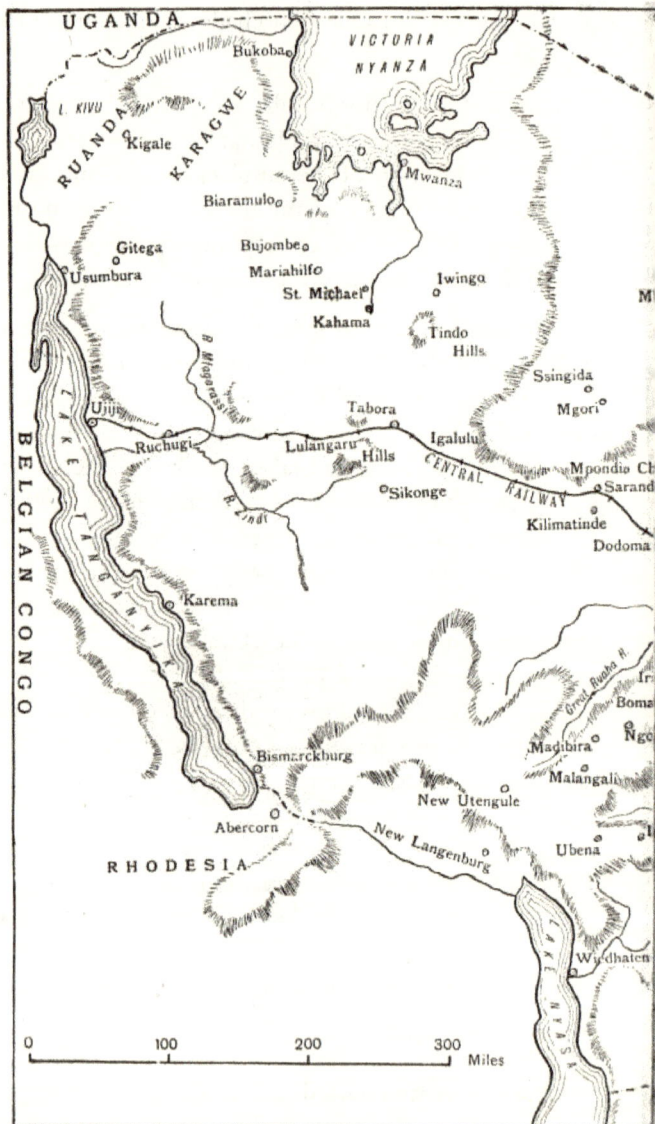

UGANDA

VICTORIA
NYANZA

L. KIVU
Bukoba

RUANDA
Kigale

KARAGWE
Mwanza

Biaramulo

Gitega
Bujombe
Mariahilf
Usumbura
St. Michael
Iwingo
Kahama

Tindo
Hills
Ssingida
Mgori

R. Moga
Tabora
Ujiji
Igalulu
Ruchugi
Lulangaru
Hills
Mpondia Ch
Sarand
CENTRAL RAILWAY
Sikonge
Kilimatinde
Dodoma

BELGIAN CONGO

LAKE TANGANYIKA

Karema

Great Ruaha R.
Ir
Boma

Madibira
Ngo
Bismarckburg
Malangali

New Utengule

Abercorn
New Langenburg
Ubena

RHODESIA

Wiedhafen
LAKE NYASA

0   100   200   300
Miles

German

UGANDA RAILWAY

Longido

Mt. Kilimanjaro
Mbuyuni Voi
Aruschao Kahe Tav
Lol Kissale Pare Mtns
Massai
Steppe Wilhelmstal Usumbara Jassin
Kondoa Momba Mts
Irangi Mkalamo Pangan R
Aneti Ssangeni Handeni
Tissakwa Meda
Naju Rugusi
Membe Nguru Mts. Sadani
Njangaio Manga ZANZIBAR
Tschunjo Mhonda R Wami
Mpapua Dakawa Bagamoyo
Kidete Msagora Mkata Mkessa
Kilossa Dar-es Salaam
Uleia Morogoro Matombo
Uluguru Tulo Manero mango
Kikumi Mtns Kongo Mkamba
Kissaki Kissangire Kissegesse
Kidodi Koge Mafia
Likinindas Ruaha R Rufji R
Muhangu Ulanga R Ntumbi Mtns.
Lukulin Ngarambi
Mahenge Madaba Kilwa
Mpotora Matandu R
Luwegu R
Liwale Lindi
Sudi Bay
Mikindani
Kionga
Ssongea Newala Majembi
Tunduru
Marumha
Rovuma R

PORTUGUESE EAST AFRICA

INDIAN OCEAN

Pembæ
Tanga

st Africa.

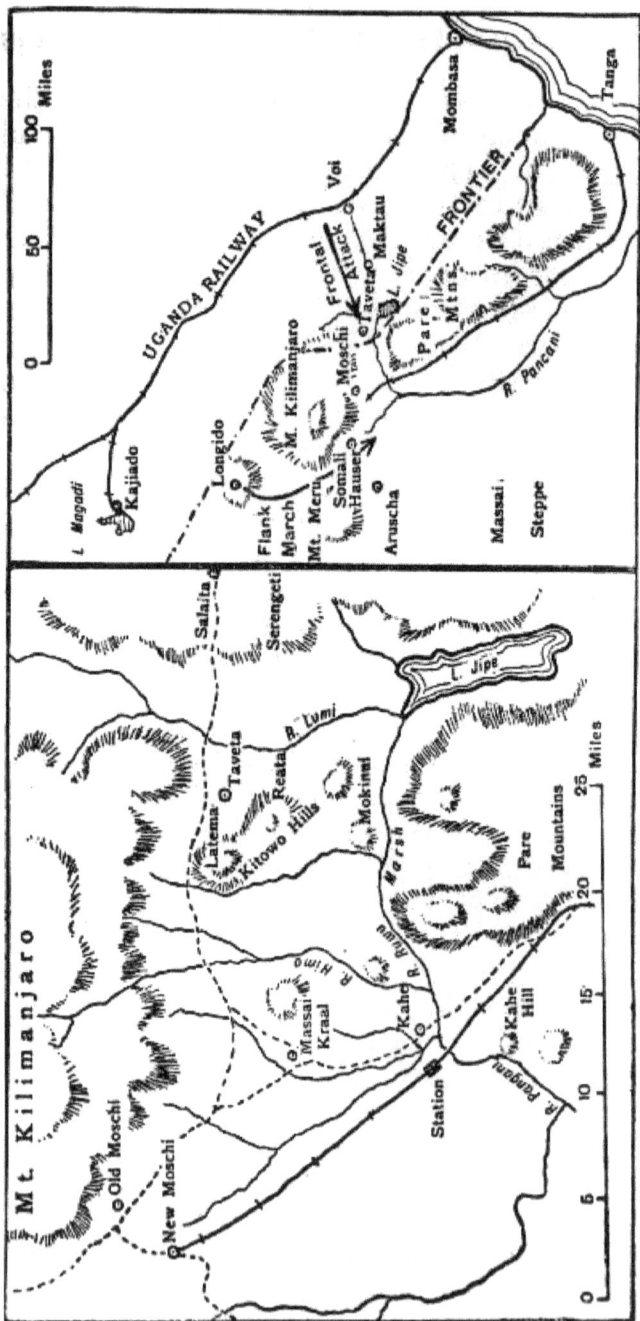

The Forcing of the Kilimanjaro Gap.

The Kilimanjaro Gap.

Sketch showing relation of the Gap to the frontier region,

Taveta reached on the 10th. The enemy made a stand in the pass of the Kitowo hills between Latema and Reata, and after a long struggle was driven out by the 2nd Division on the night of the 11th. On the 12th Van Deventer, moving on the skirts of Kilimanjaro, crossed the Himo River, and on the 13th reached New Moschi, the railway terminus. On the 15th he was in Old Moschi, higher up in the hills. On the 14th the 1st Division reached New Moschi, while the 2nd Division held a line from the Latema Pass to the Himo. The enemy position in the gap had been turned, and he was retreating towards the Ruwu and the Tanga Railway.

The next step was to secure the Ruwu crossings, and to do it in time to intercept the retreat of his main body; but there was much difficult broken country between us and the river. Van Deventer was ordered to march by night and cross the Pangani south of Kahe station, so as to get in rear of the enemy's position, while the 1st Division advanced direct on the Ruwu. By daylight on the 21st Van Deventer was fording the Pangani, and presently had seized Kahe hill. He then occupied the station, while the enemy blew up the railway bridge. This cut off von Lettow's retreat by the railway west of the Pare range, and the only hope for the Germans on the Ruwu was the Lake Jipe route east of the mountains.

If the 1st Division, now under General Sheppard, could but ford the Ruwu in time, a comprehensive disaster would follow. At 11.30 a.m. on the 21st Sheppard was pressing forward; but the Germans fought stubborn rear-guard actions, and in the thick bush progress was slow. That night the enemy slipped across the Ruwu, and so saved his retirement by Lake Jipe. On the same day, the 21st, Aruscha, fifty miles west of Moschi, was occupied by a party of Van Deventer's scouts. The pass had been forced, the whole area north of the Ruwu was cleared, and a base in enemy country had been won before the rains for the next move forward. The great mountain, whose chief peak bore the name of the German Emperor, was in our hands. The commander-in-chief moved his headquarters to Moschi, and prepared for the second stage.

It was now the end of March, but still the rains tarried. General Smuts made all possible haste to improve his communications against the wet weather by pushing on the railway from Voi across the Lumi to link up with the Tanga line. He relied mainly on motor transport, and, once the rains began, that would be useless. He effected a complete reorganisation of this command, abolishing the old two divisions

MULE DRAWN ARTILLERY

and disposing his troops in three divisions—two made up wholly of South African contingents, and one containing the Indian and British forces. Under the new arrangement the 1st Division, under Major-General Hoskins, comprised the 1st East African Brigade, under Brigadier-General Sheppard, and the 2nd East African Brigade, under Brigadier-General Hannyngton.

The 2nd Division, under Major-General Van Deventer, contained the 1st South African Mounted Brigade, under Brigadier General Manie Botha, and the 3rd South African Infantry Brigade, under Brigadier-General C. A. L. Berrange. The 3rd Division, under Major-General Brits, had the 2nd South African Mounted Brigade, under Brigadier-General Enslin, and the 2nd South African Infantry Brigade, under Brigadier-General Beves.

This done, the commander-in-chief considered his next step. Reviewing the various possibilities, he concluded that the main enemy force had retired into the Pare and Usambara mountains, expecting to be followed. He resolved to disappoint them, and to strike at the unguarded interior. He would send Van Deventer with the 2nd Division straight towards Kondoa Irangi, which would compel von Lettow to weaken his force in the mountains and on the Tanga line, and enable the other two divisions, he hoped, to conquer the ranges.

To this decision he was helped by the fact that the coming rainy season would be worst in the mountain area, and that if he moved swiftly south he need not bring operations to a standstill during April and May. Meantime, he arranged that the 2,000 British rifles under Lieutenant-Colonel Adye on Lake Victoria, and the large Belgian forces around Lake Kivu, should begin to press in from the western border.

Van Deventer started from Aruscha on 3rd April, and that night captured the hill and wells of Lol Kissale, thirty-five miles to the south. Starting again on the 8th, his horsemen arrived at Tarangire on the 9th, and at Ufiome on the 12th. He was now more than half-way to his goal, but the rains had begun, and progress was difficult. His horses were greatly exhausted, and it was not till the 17th that touch was found with the main enemy position, four miles north of Kondoa Irangi. At noon on the 19th the place fell.

It was a magnificent forced march, involving severe privations and immense fatigue. The incessant rain had made cooking impossible; there had been no rations, and the men had lived on scraps of meat and meal, and the animals on mealie stalks and grass. The 2nd Division

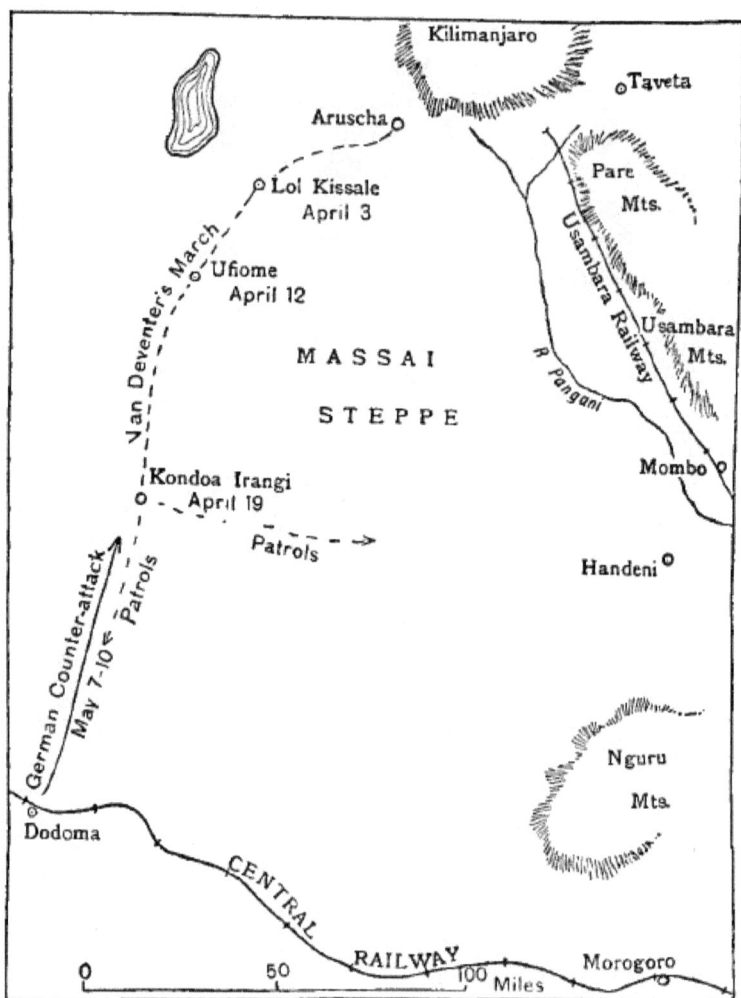

Van Deventer's March towards the Central Railway.

had come to the end of its tether, and Van Deventer had to wait for remounts before he could move.

The most he could do was to push out patrols towards the Central Railway in the south and Handeni in the east. He was cut loose from his base, and had to live on local supplies; which, fortunately, were plentiful, for the Kondoa Irangi plateau was full of cattle and renowned for its fertility. The capture of the place had seriously discomposed the enemy. Von Lettow moved a force of 4,000 from the Usambara Mountains by way of Mombo, Morogoro, and Dodoma, and on the 7th of May attacked Van Deventer's 3,000 weary troops from the south. By the 10th the attack had a been beaten off, and no further serious offensive was attempted by von Lettow during the campaign. Van Deventer's march to Kondoa Irangi was, strategically perhaps, the most significant episode in the campaign, as it was certainly the most picturesque.

A few days later the 1st and 3rd Divisions began their advance down the Tanga Railway, the first force of the rains having slackened and the ground hardened. General Smuts's plan was to move eastward to a point opposite Handeni, and then to swing south against the Central Railway on a line parallel to Van Deventer's. It was essential to move fast, while the enemy was still vainly battling at Kondoa Irangi. There were large German forces in the Pare and Usambara mountains; but General Smuts hoped to march down the Pangani (which flows twenty miles south of the hills), and to occupy Handeni before reinforcements could reach it from the west and north. It was the boldest kind of plan, for he condemned his main body to move through dense bush with an unfordable river on its right.

In that advance went Sheppard's and Beves's brigades, (General Brits, of the 3rd Division, did not arrive till the end of June), while as flank guards Hannyngton's brigade of Indian troops moved along the railway just under the hills; and the 3rd King's African Rifles, under Lieutenant-Colonel Fitzgerald, made a circuit north of the Pare range in order to descend on the railway through the Ngulu gap.

Von Lettow's *askaris* knew the country well, but we had in our service many old Boer and British hunters who had as much bush lore as any native. These men did brilliant work in that difficult descent of the Pangani valley. Fitzgerald started on 18th May; Hannyngton's brigade and the main column on the 22nd. On the 25th Hannyngton had occupied Same station, and next day Fitzgerald joined him through the Ngulu gap. This turned the enemy's first position at Lembini, which

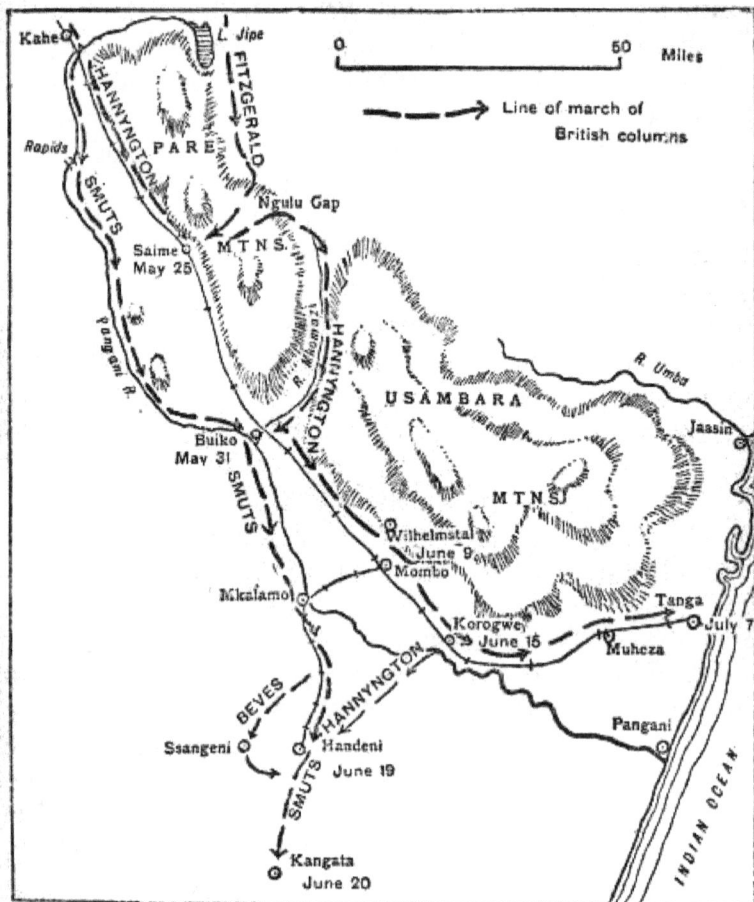

The March down the Pangani.

was taken by Hoskins without a blow. On the 31st of May Buiko station, where the Pangani and the railway meet, was occupied, and the enemy was in retreat to Mombo, whence ran a trolley line to Handeni. This made it clear that the Germans were not going to defend the Usambara range, but were retiring by Handeni to the Central Railway. To Hannyngton was left the task of clearing the near end of those hills, which he did by advancing to Mombo on the 9th of June, occupying Wilhelmstal (the summer seat of the German Government) on the 12th, and reaching Korogwe on the 15th. The main force had meantime crossed to the right bank of the Pangani. Beves's brigade executed a turning movement towards the west by Ssangeni, while Sheppard's brigade on the 19th entered Handeni itself. Next day he was joined by Hannyngton from Korogwe.

In Handeni we had a second strategic base, parallel to Kondoa Irangi, for our advance on the Central Railway; and now that we held it, the enemy at Kondoa was wholly cut off from the north. General Smuts's line of communication was getting very long, for he had not yet opened up another sea base, and rations and comforts were terribly short among his wearied men. But the indefatigable spirit of the commander-in-chief was communicated to the army, and he was able to induce them to still further exertions when it seemed that they had already passed the limit of their strength. From a military point of view, he was right to press on, for delay might lose him the fruit of his remarkable successes.

On the 20th he moved to Kangata, for he heard that the enemy was in position on the Lukigura River. A column under Hoskins was dispatched in a flanking movement, while Sheppard attacked in front, and on the 24th the line was won. Here, perforce, a halt must be called. Since 22nd May the troops had marched over 200 miles in desperate country, and the transport system had reached the extreme radius of its capacity. The Nguru range of mountains lay before us, and it appeared that there the enemy was massing in force. Moreover, it was desirable to bring Van Deventer and the 2nd Division farther forward to conform with the advance of the main force, before a combined movement could be undertaken against the Central Railway. Accordingly, a big standing camp was formed on the Msiha River, eight miles beyond the Lukigura, and just under the north-east buttress of the Nguru hills.

The enemy had virtually evacuated the Usambara hills, and on 7th July Tanga was occupied, with the help of the Navy, almost with-

General Hamyngton in East Africa interrogating a German native porter guarded by Indian sepoys

out opposition. Small guerilla bands still hung around the Korogwe neighbourhood; but during July the country was cleared by an advance from Tanga and Pangani, and by a movement of Hannyngton from the south. To complete our hold on the north, Sadani Bay was occupied by our navy on 1st August, and Bagamoyo on the 15th, and the way was thus prepared for the larger advance on Dar-es-Salaam.

On the western marches the Belgians, under General Tombeur, having moved their base from Kibati, north of Lake Kivu, to Bukakate, on Lake Victoria, had occupied Kigali, the capital of the Ruanda province, and the British "Lake detachment" had taken the island of Ukerewe, in Lake Victoria. Sir Charles Crewe was now appointed to the Lake command, and occupied during June the Bukoba and Karagwe districts of Ruanda. On 14th July he compelled the enemy to evacuate Mwanza, his most important town on the lake, and so won a valuable base for a future movement on Tabora. The readiness with which the enemy gave up this area compelled General Smuts to revise his views. He had formerly thought that Tabora would be the goal of von Lettow's retreat; he now reached the conclusion that it would either be south-eastwards to the Rufiji delta, or south to the Mahenge plateau.

The Msiha camp was an uneasy resting-place. The enemy in the mountains to the south kept up a persistent shelling, and the troops had to burrow for shelter into the ground. But the halt was of immense advantage, for it enabled weary units to rest, and allowed us to collect reserves of supplies and to receive reinforcements from South Africa of both guns and infantry. Meanwhile Van Deventer had begun to move on 24th June, in order to come into line with the rest of the army, and to co-operate in reducing the Nguru position. He broke up the enemy's lines south of Kondoa, which had already been weakened by the transference of troops to Nguru. His immediate objective was now the Central Railway; but his advance was so arranged that it should also have a bearing on the Nguru situation, and intercept the main enemy force as they fell back from the hills. On 20th July a column moved westward and occupied Ssingida.

On 14th July a column started due south, and after a stiff encounter at Mpondi reached Saranda and Kilimatinde, and so got astride the Central Railway. Van Deventer's main forces advanced to the southeast, the mounted brigade under Manie Botha being diverted on Kikombo, and Berrange's infantry by way of Njangalo upon Dodoma. Njangalo was reached on 25th July and Kikombo on the 30th. The end of July saw a hundred miles of the Central Railway in our pos-

BRITISH ARMY ARTILLERY

session, and though every bridge and culvert had been destroyed, the enemy had not had time to do serious damage to the track.

The much-tried 2nd Division had done marvels, but its precarious line of supply from Moschi had now been lengthened by another 100 miles, and its next objective, Kilossa, was a further 120 miles on. Nevertheless, with scarcely a halt, it pushed down the railway. It partially solved its transport problem by narrowing the gauge of its heavy lorries, so that they could run on railway trolley wheels. Mpapua was taken on 12th August, Kidete on the 16th, and Kilossa on the 22nd. During July, too, the Belgians and the British Lake detachment had been steadily drawing near to Tabora. Ujiji and Kigoma, on the shores of Tanganyika, had been occupied, and Ruchugi, on the line to Tabora; while from the north-west a column was approaching St. Michael. General Northey, in the south-west, had taken Malangali, and was moving on Iringa. Von Lettow had now but one direction of retreat left to him—the south.

It was time for General Smuts's main force to advance and clear the Nguru hills. The mountain region was some fifty miles long from north to south, and about twenty-five miles broad, and had on the north-east a subsidiary feature in the shape of Mount Kanga, between which and the Nguru *massif* the Mdjonga River flowed south to join the Wami. It was a region of narrow wooded defiles, rushing streams, and tracks winding on the edge of precipices—an ideal country for any defensive. General Smuts's plan was to send Sheppard's brigade against the main Kanga position, while Hannyngton's brigade advanced on its right down the Mdjonga valley on Matamondo and Turiani. Brits's 3rd Division was ordered to fetch a circuit round the north end of the mountains, and close in upon Mdondo from the west.

Brits started on 5th August, Hannyngton on the 6th, and Sheppard on the 7th. Sheppard feinted against the main enemy front at Kanga, but his left wing moved six miles east so as to turn the mountain and come in on the enemy rear at the Russongo River. Enslin, with the mounted troops of Brits's division, occupied Mdondo on the 8th; but reported that the hill roads were impossible for wheeled traffic, with the result that all the transport had to be sent back to the Lukiguru to follow Sheppard.

Hannyngton reached Matamondo on the 9th, where he found himself strongly opposed. Beves's brigade was accordingly sent to support him, and meantime Enslin at Mdondo was threatening the enemy's rear and compelling him to think of retreat.

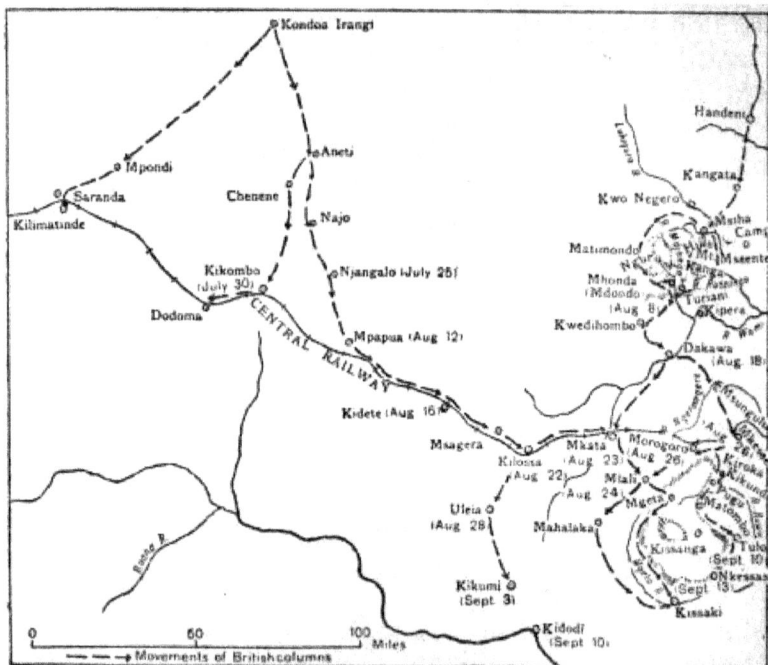

The Advance across the Central Railway.

Had the whole 3rd Division been able to reach Mdondo, the Mata-mondo force might have been cut off. As it was, after severe fighting on the 10th and 11th, that force fell back, and on the 11th Sheppard reached the Russongo River, to find the enemy gone. He then marched south to Kipera, on the river Wami, while Brits and Hannyngton reached Turiani. By the 15th Brits and Hannyngton were clear of the Nguru hills, and on the 18th the whole British force was at Dakawa, at the crossing of the Wami. The enemy was retreating partly on Kilossa, but mainly on Morogoro. On the 22nd, as we have seen, Van Deventer reached Kilossa, so Morogoro became the only refuge.

General Smuts had hopes of bringing von Lettow to bay at Morogoro, and denying him retreat to the south. The place, which stands on a tributary of the Ngerengere, was protected from the Dakawa direction by a long line of hills, and had the Uluguru mountains behind it. To force him to fight, General Smuts devised an elaborate outflanking plan. Enslin, with the 2nd Mounted Brigade, was to make for the Central Railway at Mkata, to cut off the outlet to the west; while the main force marched south-east, in order to approach Morogoro by way of the Ngerengere valley, and to cut the enemy's retreat to the east by Kiroka.

Enslin duly reached Mkata on the 23rd and Mlali on the 24th, where he received in support the 1st Mounted Brigade, now under Brigadier General Nussey, from Van Deventer's 2nd Division. Unfortunately, there was a track, unknown to us, which led due south from Morogoro through the mountains to Kissaki, and by this way von Lettow escaped. On the 24th we reached the Ngerengere, on the 26th Hannyngton was at Mkesse, on the east, and the same day Sheppard entered Morogoro. But the enemy had gone, and gone precipitately, to judge by burning storehouses and the railway platform deep in spilt coffee.

General Smuts, though both men and animals were well-nigh worn out, pressed hard on his trail. On the 27th Sheppard was in Kiroka, and by the 30th the enemy was behind the little river Ruwu. The struggle for the Uluguru range was one of the hardest in the campaign. Brits's 3rd Division moved on the west side, with Enslin's Mounted Brigade on his left among the hills, while Hoskins's 1st Division took the eastern flank. Von Lettow fought stout rear-guard actions, excellently supported by the nature of the country.

General Smuts wrote:

The road passes through very difficult broken foothills, covered either with bush or grass growing from six to twelve feet high, through which any progress was slow, painful, and difficult. The bridging of the Ruwu took several days, and for some distance beyond the road passes along the face of precipitous rocks round which the enemy had constructed a gallery on piles to afford a track for his transport. As the gallery would not carry our mechanical transport, it took us some days to blast away the mountain side and construct a proper road.

Tulo was not reached till 10th September, and Hannyngton, who led the vanguard, drove the enemy south of the Mgeta River on the 13th. It was clear, from the heavy gun ammunition left behind, that von Lettow had contemplated an elaborate defence of the Uluguru range; but the speed of the 1st Division, and the unexpected appearance of Enslin's troops at Mlali, had forced him to change his plans. Brits and Enslin followed the elephant track by Mahalaka which Speke and Burton had taken in 1857. On the 5th of September they were close on Kissaki, and it was decided to attack the place with Beves's infantry brigade, Enslin's mounted brigade of the 3rd Division, and Nussey's mounted brigade of the 2nd Division, which had been lent to Brits.

The attack failed, because it was badly timed, the three units did not act together, and the thick bush prevented assistance being sent from one to the other. It was not till the 15th of September that, Hannyngton having taken Dutumi, eighteen miles to the east, Enslin managed to outflank the position and threaten the retreat to the Rufiji. The enemy fell back on a defensive line along the Mgeta River.

During this period of hard fighting astride the Central Railway, the situation on the coast was being rapidly improved. Brigadier-General Edwards, the Inspector-General of Communications, moved south from Bagamoyo with two columns, one along the Ruwu River towards the Central Railway, and the other direct on Dar-es-Salaam. British warships appeared off the coast, and on 3rd September the German capital surrendered. The time had now come to occupy the whole coast, and, with the assistance of the Navy, Mikindani was seized on 13th September, Ssudi Bay on the 15th, Lindi on the 16th, and Kilwa and Kilwa Kissiwani on the 7th.

Kilwa was an important base, and a strong column was landed there for operations along the Matandu River and in the Mtumbi mountains. Dar-es-Salaam was also a vital centre, and from it the work

Von Lettow on campaign

of restoring the eastern end of the railway, most comprehensively wrecked by the Germans, was carried on. Between the sea and Kilossa our Pioneer Corps had to rebuild no less than sixty bridges.

At the same time Van Deventer was not idle. On 28th August he had taken Uleia, and by 3rd September was at Kikumi. On the 10th he was at Kidodi, on the Great Ruaha River, where he found the enemy in position. General Northey, too, had occupied Lupembe on 19th August and Iringa on the 29th, and was moving upon the Mahenge plateau from the west; while on the south he had taken Ssongea, eighteen miles east of Wiedhafen, on Lake Nyasa. Farther north Sir Charles Crewe and General Tombeur were converging on Tabora, which was entered by the Belgians on 19th September. The German garrison there fell back towards the upper waters of the Great Ruaha, where they had to face both Van Deventer and Northey.

One other episode remains to be mentioned. On 9th of March Portugal, the oldest ally of Britain, had declared war on Germany. Her main military effort was to be on the Flanders front, where presently she had two divisions in line with the British. But since her colony of Mozambique bordered German East Africa on the south, she played some small part also in this campaign. Her troops, under General Gil, crossed the frontier, the Rovuma River, and occupied various points on its northern shore. As it was evident that von Lettow's retreat would be to the southward, the Portuguese forces must sooner or later come into action.

The position at the end of September was that in little more than six months the German hold on East Africa had been narrowed down to the area between the Rufiji and Mgeta Rivers in the northeast, and the Great Ruaha and Ulanga Rivers in the south-west. Outside this area the enemy's only troops were the Tabora garrison, now making its painful way eastward, and a small detachment between Dar-es-Salaam and the Rufiji. With the exception of the Mahenge plateau, he had lost every healthy district of the colony. He was dwelling now in fever swamps, while the bulk of our troops were on higher ground.

But General Smuts's gallant forces were woefully exhausted, and far from comfortable in the way of supplies. The fighting front was fed from the railhead at Korogwe, west of Tanga, and everything had to be brought 300 miles by hill paths and bush tracks. Often the ration problem became acute. At Kissaki, for example, a sudden storm of rain destroyed the roads, and for a fortnight our troops there lived off native millet and the flesh of hippos shot in the Mgeta River. "Fly" had played havoc with our transport animals, and large numbers of men were down with malaria. The 3rd Division had to be sent back to Morogoro to recover strength; and though we harassed the enemy on the Mgeta line, major operations were for the time being at an end.

The rest of the campaign, it was evident, would be in an unhealthy country, and it was necessary to have medical reports on the fitness of the troops. As a result, 12,000 men were sent back to South Africa as unfit for further campaigning. By way of reinforcements, the Loyal North Lancashires returned from the Cape at full strength, and the Nigerian Brigade, under Brigadier-General Cunliffe, arrived in November. It was calculated that by the end of the year the worst part of the transport difficulties would be overcome by the opening of the Central Railway for traffic between Dar-es-Salaam and Dodoma. The enemy's main force lay facing us north of the Rufiji, and if compelled to retire, he must fall back either on Mahenge or into Portuguese territory.

To force the crossing of the Rufiji was no light task, for it was more than a quarter of a mile wide. General Smuts's aim was to cut off the Rufiji force from Mahenge, and at the same time prevent their retirement to the south. Accordingly, he established a base at Kilwa, on the coast, from which columns could work north and north-west. He hoped to cross the Rufiji somewhere well to the west of Kibambawe, in order to bar the road to Mahenge and then join hands with the Kilwa column, so as to close in on the enemy's rear.

General Hannyngton yielded up the command of the 2nd East African Brigade to Colonel O'Grady, and took over the Kilwa force, which was now called the 3rd East African Brigade. There were other changes. The 3rd Division was disbanded, the Lake detachment ceased to exist, Van Deventer's command was reorganised, and reinforcements were sent to Northey.

The situation in the area of the last-named during October became interesting, for the Tabora garrison succeeded in breaking through and cutting the communications between Northey's main body and the Iranga troops. A small British post at Ngominji was surrounded and taken prisoner. There were various minor actions at Madibira, Malingali, and Lupembe, in which the enemy lost heavily. In November General Smuts visited that area, and instructed Van Deventer to base himself on Iringa and Northey on Lupembe, and between them force the enemy beyond the Ruhudje and Ulanga Rivers. Meantime Hannyngton at Kilwa had done good work in clearing the Matandu valley and the southern slopes of the Mtumbi mountains.

145

GERMAN BATTLE LINE

In November the whole 1st Division, less Sheppard's brigade, was transferred to Kilwa, with General Hoskins in command. There during December there was a good deal of fighting, but by the close of the year Hoskins felt himself in a position to advance towards the Lower Rufiji when our main forces should attack. Meantime the Portuguese were driven off the north bank of the Rovuma, and it was clear that if von Lettow broke out in that direction he would meet with no serious opposition.

The great advance was ordered for New Year's Day, 1917. The plan of it was that Beves's brigade should move to the west and cross the Rufiji just below its junction with the Ruaha, and that Sheppard and Cunliffe should make a similar flanking movement on the east. The vital part was that of Beves. On the night of the 2nd he was only twelve miles from the great river, and at dawn on the 3rd had crossed and established a bridgehead on the southern bank. On the 5th Sheppard, after hard fighting, in which the most famous of African hunters, Captain F. C. Selous, fell at the head of his company, reached Kibambawe, to find that the enemy had crossed after destroying the bridge.

That night he managed to effect a crossing a little higher up, in the course of which he had to deal with some truculent hippos, and next night the passage was continued till the 30th Punjabis were established on the south shore. Beves meanwhile was making good his hold as far as Luhembero, and Cunliffe's brigade was ordered to follow him. The enemy had been completely outmanoeuvred, and with few casualties we had won the Rufiji crossing.

The situation now was that the Tabora garrison had slipped away from both Northey and Van Deventer, and was making for Mahenge, while von Lettow had got across the Rufiji without being forced to action. It showed the impossibility of surrounding an enemy in such country; he could be driven in, but not brought to a standstill. Meantime Hoskins's force from Kilwa was steadily advancing to the north-west. General Smuts, reviewing the situation, saw that between Cunliffe on the Rufiji and Hannyngton at Ngarambi there was a gap of some forty miles, the only outlet through which the enemy could escape. If the two could join hands at Lugaliro the trap might be closed. Failing such a success, there must be a converging movement from the Rufiji and Kilwa upon Liwale in the south.

But General Smuts was not suffered to conclude the campaign which he had devised. He was summoned to England to the Imperial War Conference, and left Dar-es-Salaam on the 26th of January.

L. Kwa

Bukoba
VICTORIA
NYANZA

KARAGWE

RUANDA

Kigale BELGIANS

Mwanza
July 14

BELGIAN ADVANCE
July Sept St. Michael's
Iwingo

Lake detachm

BELGIAN CONGO

Ssingi
July 20
Ko

Ujiji

BELGIANS
Tabora
Sept. 19

Central Railway

Ruchugi

BELGIANS

LAKE TANGANYIKA

Karema

Frontier

Bismarckburg

NORTHERN

Abercorn

RHODESIA

0   100   200   300
                              Miles

— — — Movements of the Allies

East Africa.—Sketch showin
opera

g the general scheme of the
itions.

Von Lettow's Schutztrupe on the March

The new Commander-in-Chief was Lieutenant-General Hoskins, formerly of the 1st Division. With his accession to command the campaign took on a new phase. The main problem had been solved; the country had been virtually conquered; all the main centres were in our hands; the worst transport difficulties had been surmounted; and the enemy had become a hunted remnant. But the colony was not yet cleared, and it was to take many weary months before the last man of von Lettow's following crossed the Rovuma. The difficulty now was that, with the exception of Mahenge, there were no such strategical objectives as had been offered by Moschi, Tabora, or Dar-es-Salaam. The campaign had become a man-hunt, a chase of a new De Wet, with difficulties to face which no British commander had dreamed of in 1902.

The operations of 1917 may be briefly summarised. During January the central forces advanced east and south from the Rufiji, where the enemy fought stubborn rear-guard actions, while the Kilwa force pushed west into the Rufiji delta from Mohoro, and Northey drove the enemy from the high ground east of Lupembe. The situation remained unchanged during the rains—the longest and heaviest ever known in that country—save that under our pressure there was a steady trickling of German troops southwards both from the Rufiji and Mahenge. In the beginning of May the enemy was in two main bodies—one between 4,000 and 5,000 strong, under von Lettow himself, in the Matandu valley, to which had been added the troops driven out of the Rufiji delta; and one under Tafel, some 2,000 or 3,000 strong, based on Mahenge.

Occasionally, and especially in the west, oddments broke back northward, and these were pursued and accounted for by our mounted men. One isolated party, foraging in search of food, had reached Portuguese territory; and one large body, 600 strong, under a certain Naumann, gave more trouble north of the Central Railway, and was not disposed of till October. These raiders covered in their travels about 2,000 miles, having started from the Nyasa neighbourhood in February, and passed through Itunda, crossing the railway east of Tabora in May. They had a brush with the Belgians east of Lake Victoria, and then visited in turn Lake Magadi, Kondoa Irangi, Handeni, and Moschi, being finally brought to bay in the middle of the Massai *steppe*.

Naumann was a brutal scoundrel, but his enterprise was a bold one. General Van Deventer wrote:

Column of East African Mounted Rifles

Such a raid could perhaps only have been carried out in a country like German East Africa, where the bush is often so thick that two considerable forces may pass within a mile unaware of each other's presence, and where a ruthless leader of a small force can nearly always live on the country.

Van Deventer took over the supreme command from General Hoskins at the end of May. He himself led the main army against von Lettow's eastern force; while Northey, with the assistance of a Belgian contingent, closed in on Tafel's western force in the Mahenge area, shepherding northwards the bands that were making for Portuguese Nyasaland. In July there was hard fighting in the Kilwa district, and von Lettow was slowly driven south from the Matandu River towards Lindi. Early in October the Belgians occupied the Mahenge plateau, and moved southward in touch with our troops advancing from the west. The doom of Tafel's western detachment was now assured. It tried to join hands with von Lettow by going east through the wild country north of the Rovuma; but on 26th November Tafel discovered that his way was barred. He attempted to break back, failed, and on 28th November surrendered unconditionally.

By the beginning of the same month von Lettow was driven south-west of Lindi. There was no other course before him but precipitate flight, and moving with great speed, he reached the Rovuma, where the Portuguese posts were of no avail to hold him. With some 2,000 men he crossed the river on 25th and 26th November, and the colony of German East Africa was clear of its former masters. The ten months since General Smuts's departure had been no less a trial of fortitude than the ten months of his command. The weather had been bad, sickness was rife, and "a brigade which could put 1,400 rifles into the firing-line considered itself singularly fortunate."

Between May and November, the British casualties in action alone had been close on 6,000; but, to set against these, 1,618 Germans and 5,482 natives had been killed or captured. It had been a bitter struggle, and before it ceased nine-tenths of the enemy's white and black personnel had either perished or been taken prisoner. General Van Deventer wrote:

My predecessors have well described the difficulties of advancing through tropical Africa against an enemy in possession of interior lines who can advance and retire along carefully prepared lines of supply. As the area of operations diminished, so

ASKARIS GOING INTO ACTION

the potential advantages of these interior lines increased, and the fiercer became the fighting. The morale of the enemy never wavered, and nothing but the determined gallantry and endurance of our troops finally crushed him. To the infantry—British, South African, Indian, West and East African—I owe unqualified thanks and praise, and especially to the regimental officers who set an example which all have followed.

The campaign in German East Africa must rank as unique among the operations of the Great War. It was the most colossal "drive" ever undertaken in modern warfare, having regard both to the size of the country and the intricacy of its configuration. In it the fantastic was of daily occurrence. Outposts driven in by lions, river crossings confused by nervous hippos, engagements with the enemy disorganized by impartial attacks of rhinos against both sides—where else could such incidents be found? It was a blending of the hoar-ancient and the ultra-modern—airplanes, barbed wire, and machine guns, with the staked pit which had been the device of Neolithic man. And as a background it had the brooding terrors of the equatorial climate, death lurking in pool and swamp, in arid bush and ferny ravine, on mountain lawn and in lush valley.

From the military point of view, it was a remarkable performance, and the credit belonged to both combatants. The young Staff officer from Posen showed a true genius for war, far greater than that of many belauded German generals in Europe. He played what cards he possessed with masterly skill and a supreme patience. On the British side the task was akin to that in South-West Africa and in the Cameroons, but the harder inasmuch as the country was larger and more inaccessible and the enemy better prepared.

No campaign in tropical lands in British history had offered so difficult a problem, for in none had the enemy possessed highly-trained European officers. In transport difficulties alone, it outdistanced all our former expeditions on the Indian border, in West Africa, or on the Nile. Indeed, it combined the difficulties both of a civilized and a savage war. We had to face modern weapons and modern strategy; but a decision could not be secured merely by defeating the enemy, for he could fade away into dim forests, and find shelter in the ancient inorganic barbarism of the land.

The chief credit belongs to General Smuts, and the reason of his achievement was that he put his whole soul into it, that he treated it

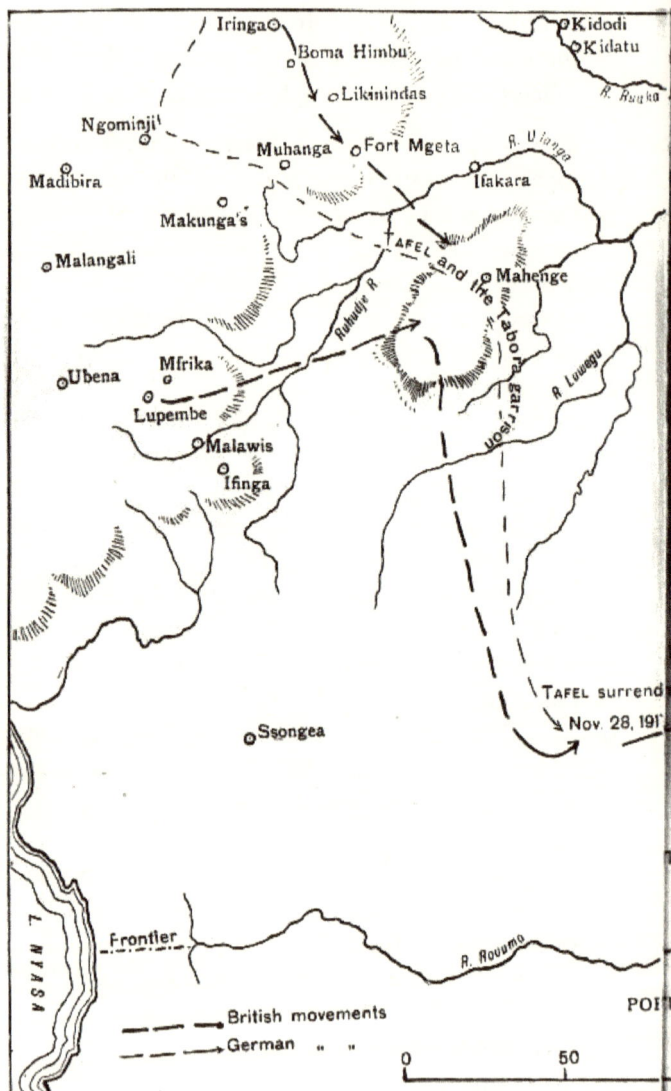

The Operations in the South-East of Germ[an...]
(Only the general direction[s...]

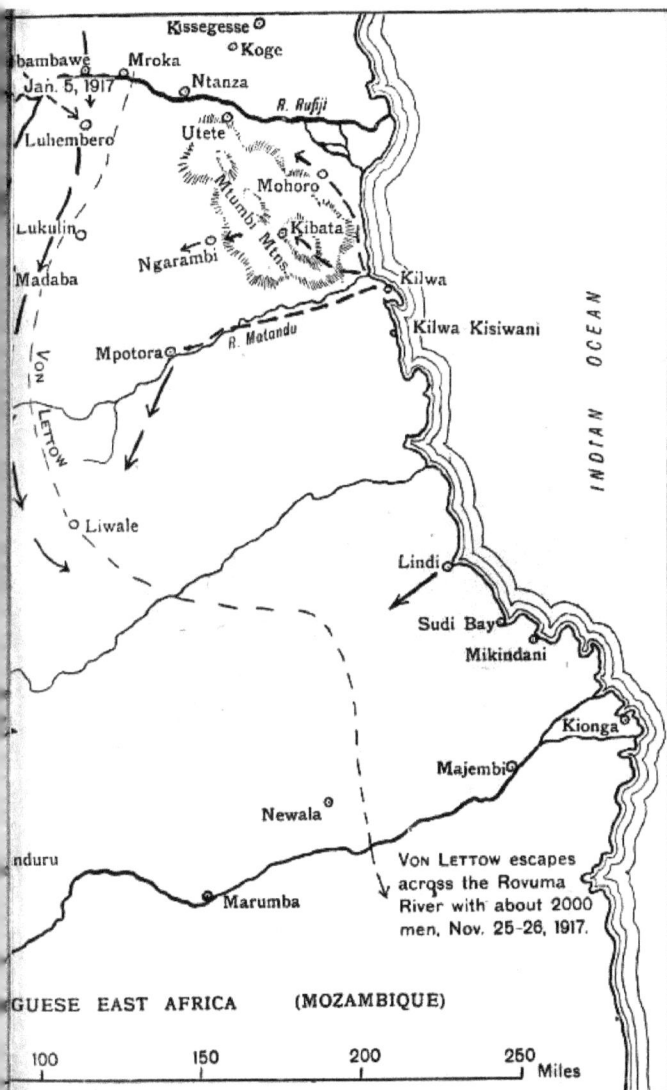

Kissegesse

Koge

bambawe   Mroka

Jan. 5, 1917   Ntanza

R. Rufiji

Luhembero   Utete

Mohoro

Lukulin   Mtumbi Mtns.   Kibata

Madaba   Ngarambi   Kilwa

VON   Mpotora   R. Matandu   Kilwa Kisiwani

LETTOW

INDIAN OCEAN

Liwale

Lindi

Sudi Bay

Mikindani

Kionga

Majembi

Newala

nduru   VON LETTOW escapes
across the Rovuma
River with about 2000
Marumba   men, Nov. 25-26, 1917.

GUESE EAST AFRICA   (MOZAMBIQUE)

100   150   200   250   Miles

East Africa in the Winter of 1916 and in 1917.

the movements is indicated.)

as a major operation of the first importance, and was as resolute to complete the work as if the war had been confined to that one area. Without his fiery energy, his far-reaching strategical grasp, or his quick imagination, we should speedily have reached a stalemate; and in two years, instead of clearing the country, have advanced perhaps to the Wami, perhaps only to the Pangani. He combined all our assets and all our far-flung detachments in one closely-wrought strategical plan. He did more, for he inspired his whole command with his own magnetic spirit, and lifted it over hard places which might well have proved unconquerable without such leadership. He was the soul and brain of the army he led, and though in men like Van Deventer and Northey and Hannyngton he had most able lieutenants, it was the shaping and controlling mind at the top which made victory certain.

But he could not have succeeded but for the splendid material of his army. Its trials were of a kind to sap the courage of most men. Poor food, excessive fatigue, and constant sickness are the hardest foes for humanity to strive with, and all who are familiar with tropical Africa know the deadly lassitude which infects the blood of Europeans and takes the edge from their spirit. In two months during the autumn of 1916 the wastage of animals was: horses, 10,000; mules, 10,000; oxen, 11,000; donkeys, 2,500. In one week of the same period there were 9,000 sick in hospital, 4,000 of them white men, and over 200 officers.

Let the reader reflect what such a handicap meant for operations, and then assess the credit for those swift marches which flung the enemy from position after position, and tore river lines from his grasp before he was aware of the menace. It was a war on both sides of picked men, black and white. The Angoni of the King's African Rifles, the Manyema of the Belgians, the Wanyamwezi of the Germans, were the military *élite* of Central Africa. We had behind us famous Indian battalions; corps of settlers accustomed to fend for themselves in the wilds; scouts and hunters who had long made a dwelling in the bush; the same type of South African infantryman who in France had fought at Delville Wood and Arras; and those mounted Boers whose quality we knew well, and who among natives who had never seen a horse won a legendary fame as the "Kabure"—a new animal brought forth by the war.

Their heroism and endurance were not expended on a mere side-show, for, far as East Africa seemed removed from the strategical centre of gravity, the difficulty of its conquest showed, in General Smuts's words, what an "immense tropical territory, with almost unlimited economic and military possibilities, and provided with excellent submarine bases," might become as an aid to that world empire of which Germany dreamed. And it strengthened the mind of the Allies in the resolution that:

> A land where so many of our heroes lost their lives or their health—where, under the most terrible and exacting conditions, human loyalty and human sacrifice were poured out so lavishly in a great cause—should never be allowed to become a menace to the future peaceful development of the world.

Appendix 1

The Surrender of Garua

A Memorandum sent to Sir Frederick Lugard, Governor-General of Nigeria, by an officer serving with the British Force in Cameroon, describes the surrender of Garua and its German garrison to an Anglo-French force. The memorandum, dated Garua, June 12, and issued by the Secretary for the Colonies, states:—

The unconditional surrender of Garua and its garrison—to the Allied Forces—took place the night before last without any loss of life on our side.

After a very careful reconnaissance of the whole *terrain* surrounding the enemy's positions, and having finally selected what we considered to be their weakest point of attack for our line of advance, we commenced gradually sapping by a series of parallel trenches nearer and nearer to the fort immediately to our front. Sapping only took place at night.

Bombardment of the Forts

A well-regulated bombardment of the three forts situated on the high ridge overlooking Garua, as well as on the old fort in the plain below, was kept up from heavy guns from a distance of about 4,000 yards at first, and latterly from 3,000 yards. This bombardment was supplemented on the last day or two by fire from smaller guns, for which there had been found a fairly well-concealed position about 1,900 yards from Nos. 1 and 2 forts. The enemy kept up a very lively fire from their field guns at first—in reply to our guns which fortunately only resulted in the wounding of three or four men.

To prevent the garrison breaking out, we had left a company on the hill at Bilondi—opposite Garua and on the other side of the Benue—to watch the forts opposite their position, and employed our

M.I. patrolling and watching the fords to the south-west, the French cavalry being employed doing the same to the south-east.

On the afternoon of the 10th, about 4.30 p.m., I was observing the fire of the guns, when a French *sous-officier* rushed up to me in great excitement, saying that a white flag had been hoisted from No. 3 fort, which was not visible from where I was standing. I thought the man must be mistaken, but on moving off to the left I could clearly see through my glasses several men standing up in No. 3 fort waving white flags.

White Flags Appear

This was followed up by white flags going up in all positions and in the old fort. The cease fire was ordered, and the C.O., the French Commander, and the two Staff officers galloped forward to our forward trenches about 1,000 yards from No. 1 fort. They then dismounted and walked on another few hundred yards, headed by a man carrying a white shirt on a stick to do duty for a flag. Having arrived fairly close to the enemy's position, they halted and waited events. A long pause ensued before they saw a party of horsemen under a white flag emerge from the old fort and advance in their direction.

A German officer heading this procession on getting close to them dismounted, walked forward, saluted, and stated that he wished in the name of the German *commandant* of Garua to offer the surrender of the forts, town, and garrison of Garua to the Allied Forces; but on certain conditions—namely, the garrison to march out with the honours of war, and to be allowed to proceed down south to rejoin the rest of the German forces! Our C.O. at once replied that he would listen to no terms of any sort, and that the surrender must be absolutely unconditional. The German saluted, and replied he would carry back this answer to the German *commandant*, and requested two days' grace to bring back the *commandant's* reply. Our C.O. said he would give him two hours.

Punctual almost to the minute, we saw lights advancing, and the same officer with four others appeared and stated that our terms had been accepted, but that the *commandant* hoped that all German officers would be allowed to retain their swords, and asked that the native inhabitants of the town would be protected. This was agreed to, and the four extra German officers were then told off to guide four of our "boys" to each of the three forts and to the old forts, to take over these positions till the morning. Von Cranzelheim, the *commandant*, remained in our camp that night as a hostage.

ENTRY INTO GARUA

At daybreak the next morning, leaving our camp standing, we marched into Garua, past all three forts, with all our guns and the remainder of our troops, halted in front of the Commandant's house, pulled down the German flag, and with a flourish of bugles hoisted the Union Jack and the Tricolour side by side! Our total bag—so far as I can gather up to this moment—is 37 European prisoners (nearly all officers or non-commissioned officers) and 270 native rank and file (*Schützstruppen*). Also four field guns (three intact), ten Maxim guns (five intact), and several hundred rifles not counted yet; large quantities of equipment, saddles, bridles, etc.; workshops, containing valuable armourer's, carpenter's, and blacksmith's tools; a very well-equipped hospital, with quantities of valuable medical instruments, microscopes, medicines, bandages, and even an up-to-date dentist's chair and all dentist's tools; and an immense amount of small-arm ammunition quite half a million, I should think.

POISONED SPEARS IN PITS

The old fort, a strongly fortified walled-in enclosure surrounded by a broad deep ditch, about 150 yards by 100 yards, containing bungalows, offices, and stores, seems to be full of stuff of all sorts provisions, bales of cloth and beads, and I don't know what. The walls of the fort are of mud faced with cement and bricks, about 15 ft. or 16 ft. high and 4 ft. thick, embrasured for guns, and sandbag loopholes all round. It contains underground bombproof shelters for the garrison; a deep ditch filled with upright spears surrounds it, and outside this is a 20 ft. broad barbed-wire entanglement; beyond this an abattis of felled prickly acacia trees, and outside this again a maze of 10 ft. deep circular holes cunningly covered over, with poisoned spears, stuck upright in the bottom. Every bungalow is also strongly fortified, and surrounded in the same way with barbed-wire entanglements and covered over pits.

From a short conversation with von Cranzelheim and von Dühring (the two senior officers) it appeared that their men were completely demoralised by our shell fire—melinite and lyddite. One lucky shell bursting on No. 2 fort is said to have penetrated a bombproof shelter and exploded inside, killing about 20 of them. They began mutinying and refusing to man the forts on the 9th, and on the 10th, when our bombardment was very accurate and severe, a good number of their cavalry broke loose, seized their horses and rifles, and bolted. Fortunately, the Benue has risen considerably in the last day or two. I hear one lot who got across last night were held up by a section of our company on the other side and had 17 killed. A large number have, we know, been drowned attempting to cross, and both our M.I. and the French cavalry are now in vigorous pursuit of the remainder, on the other side of the river. Several others are, we know, hiding in the village, which is an enormous one, said to contain 10,000 inhabitants. I think we can take it for granted that the Garua garrison is completely wiped out. Not a single European has escaped.

Von Dühring says that 2,000 labourers have been hard at work for over six months fortifying the place. It is almost incredible the extraordinary luck we have had in capturing it without the loss of a single life.

The whole frontier of the Yola Province is now clear, and I don't think we need fear any more raids across the Muri Province, at any rate once we begin moving.

FORMIDABLE FORTS

Later;

I have now been round all the forts surrounding Garua, and am amazed at the skill and ingenuity shown in their construction. They are most formidable works. Each fort is within a distance of 400 to 500 yards from the next, and a fairly stiff climb up the slope. Telephones connect up with the old fort, and to the *commandant's* bungalow, nearly a mile and a half away. Very little material damage from the fire of our guns is to be seen.

All guns, rifles, equipment, Maxims, and ammunition have now been collected, together with bales of cloth and beads, and they have all been divided up equally between the French and ourselves, the cloth and beads falling to our share. These have been equally divided up amongst our men as a reward for their discipline and self-restraint. Some india-rubber and silk have also been found, and our share will be kept for public revenue.

This morning there was held a full funeral parade service over the graves of Colonel Maclear and the other officers who fell in the action last August, and a large wooden cross with their names engraved on it has been erected.

163

Appendix 2

THE CONQUEST OF THE CAMEROONS

Extract from General Dobell's Despatch.

War Office, 31st May 1916.

The following Despatch has been received by the Secretary of State for War from Major-General Sir Charles M. Dobell, K.C.B., Commanding the Allied Forces in the Cameroons:—

General Headquarters,
Cameroons, 1st March 1916.

My Lord,

I have the honour to forward herewith a summary of the operations carried out by the Allied force under my command, covering the period between the capitulation of Duala, 27th September 1914, and the termination of active operations.

I have, in this despatch, endeavoured to maintain a correct perspective, remembering that our operations in this theatre of war are incomparable in magnitude to those taking place elsewhere. For purposes of comparison I may, however, add that the number of troops of both nations at my immediate disposal at the commencement of the campaign amounted to 4,300 West African native soldiers; on the 21st November 1915, this number had been increased to 9,700, including Indian troops. In these numbers the British and French forces were approximately equal.

As Your Lordship is aware, I have kept the proper authorities informed in some detail as to the proceedings and progress of the troops under my command. These despatches I have endeavoured to forward at intervals of about a fortnight; I do not, therefore, propose to enlarge on such questions as the organisation and preparation of the force placed at my disposal, nor the naval measures that were taken in a campaign to which the adjective "amphibious" may be applied in its widest sense. It is perhaps sufficient to state I fully realised, that the conquest of a country which is some 306,000 square miles in area, or roughly one and a half times the size of the German Empire, defended by a well-led and well-trained native force, plentifully supplied with machine guns, was no light task.

2. On my passage from the United Kingdom early in September 1914, I learnt at various ports of call that the operations which had taken place on the Nigerian frontier had not been as successful as had been anticipated, thus confirming my opinion that Duala, the capital and chief port of the Cameroons, must be made my immediate objective. I entertained no doubts as to the ability of the Royal Navy to overcome the difficulties and make a landing at Duala feasible, and my best hopes were realised when I was informed that H.M.S. *Challenger* could force a passage through the sunken wrecks and other obstructions in the Cameroon River, and reach a point 7,000 yards from the town. This was made possible owing to the mine sweeping and other preparatory work which had been carried out by the Royal Navy and Nigeria Marine, under the direction of Captain Fuller, R.N., H.M.S. *Cumberland.*

On my summons for the surrender of the Colony being refused, and after duly notifying the German *commandant* of my intention, I ordered a bombardment of the town to commence early on 26th September; this in combination with a land demonstration, made by way of one of the neighbouring creeks, was sufficient to induce the *commandant*, on 27th September, to surrender the towns of Duala and Bonaberi, with a small strip of land in their environs. The surrender of Duala secured us a safe and convenient base for the future absorption of German territory; further, the capture of stores, supplies, field guns, and the removal of over 400 German Europeans was a great loss to the German Field Force, whilst the seizure of the large amount of shipping and numerous small craft in the harbour was an inestimable advantage to us.

3. My first object was to consolidate the position already won, and with this object in view an Allied force was allotted the task of clearing the country up to and including the Japoma Bridge, Midland Railway, whilst a British force commenced to make headway towards Maka on the Northern Railway line. Reconnaissances by land and water were carried out with uniformly successful results. I may remark

incidentally that neither the climate nor the character of the country favoured the offensive: officers and men were exposed to the most trying conditions; incessant tropical rains, absence of roads or even paths, a country covered with the densest African forest—all contributed to the difficulties with which the troops were faced. Had it not been for the existing railways, which formed a line of advance as well as supply, it is difficult to see how progress could have been made.

The country in the immediate vicinity of Duala is perhaps typical of the greater portion of the Cameroons in which my troops have operated, excepting beyond Northern railhead where the country becomes open and, on account of its greater altitude, healthier; but all the coast line, and for some 150 miles inland, one meets the same monotonous impenetrable African forest fringed, on the coast line, by an area of mangrove swamp in varying depth.

The zone is well watered by numerous rivers, of which the Wuri, Sanaga and Njong present serious military obstacles. Once outside this belt conditions change at once, supplies and livestock are obtainable, and open grass lands are reached; the one unusual geographical feature is the Cameroon Mountain, some 13,000 feet high, which rises abruptly from the sea, its slopes clothed with valuable plantations, and on which the hill station of Buea, the former administrative capital of the Protectorate, is perched.

4. By the first week in October we had made good the country as far as Maka and the left bank of the Dibamba Creek. The Japoma railway bridge, 900 yards in length, was broken in two places, but a fine feat was performed by the French *tirailleurs* in forcing this passage under a galling rifle and machine-gun fire. The Royal Navy and Royal Marine Light Infantry also materially contributed to this success.

I now judged that I could move a force by the Wuri River on Jabassi, so as to secure Duala from any attack from the north-east; a mixed Naval and Military force, supported by armed craft, was organized and an attack was delivered on 8th October. It is regrettable that this operation was not at first successful, difficult country, novel conditions, and the fact that our native troops encountered machine-gun fire for the first time are contributory causes to failure; nevertheless, it became necessary completely to reorganise the force and repeat the operation, with the result that Jabassi was taken on 14th October. From this place a force was pushed out to Njamtan, and the country around Jabassi was cleared of the enemy.

My next objective was Edea, on which place I determined an advance should be made from three directions, two by land and one by river. Strong forces were moved from Japoma and by the Njong River to Dehane, thence by a track towards Edea. The third force proceeded by the Sanaga River; the navigation of this river is most difficult, dangerous bars hinder entrance into its mouth and sand banks obstruct the passage up to Edea. The feat performed by Commander L. W. Braithwaite, R.N., in navigating an armed flotilla on the Sanaga was a remarkable one.

Thus, the combined movement, outlined above, was entirely successful and Edea was occupied on the morning of 26th October. This result had not been achieved without hard fighting, particularly on the part of the force operating by the line of the railway. It was during the preliminary operations in this undertaking that Lieutenant Child, Director of Nigeria Marine, Commander Gray, and Captain Franqueville, of the French Army, lost their lives through the capsizing of their boat in the surf at the mouth of the Njong River—valuable lives whose losses it was difficult to replace.

5. During the latter half of October the small force under Lieut.-Colonel Haywood was continuously engaged with the enemy on the line of the Northern Railway, but had made such good progress that I was in a position to arrange for an attack on Victoria, Soppo, and Buea. As in previous operations I divided my force, part of which was moved by water to Tiko, part from Susa by Mpundu on the Mungo River, and the third portion supplied by the Royal Navy and Royal Marine Light Infantry moved by sea to Victoria. The opposition met with cannot be described as serious, but the country was very trying to troops; the energy with which our advantage was pushed appeared to demoralise the Germans, and by the 15th November we had secured Buea, with Soppo and Victoria. We inflicted considerable casualties on the enemy whilst escaping very lightly ourselves.

With the double object of striking an effective blow at the enemy and at the same time relieving the pressure on the southern frontier of Nigeria I decided to clear the whole of the Northern Railway of the enemy, and for this purpose concentrated a force at Mujuka, under command of Colonel Gorges, on 30th November. This force gradually fought its way to the North and reached Nkongsamba (railhead), which was surrendered to us on 10th December. It is worthy of remark that we took two airplanes at this place—the first machines that had ever arrived in West Africa.

The advance was continued to Dschang, which was occupied on 3rd January, and the fort destroyed; most of the hostile resistance was met with at the Nika River, but our columns rarely remained unmolested and experienced difficulties in operating in a class of country totally different to that to which they had by then become accustomed. I decided, as soon as the fort at Dschang had been destroyed, that the place should be evacuated and Nkongsamba, with its outpost at Bare, should be our most advanced position. It was unfortunate that we could not continue to hold Dschang, as our withdrawal gave a false impression to the natives and emboldened the enemy. However, with the troops at my disposal I did not feel strong enough to maintain and supply a post 55 miles north of railhead, in a difficult and mountainous country.

6. Early in 1915 the situation was as follows:—

British troops holding Duala, the Northern Railway with Bare, Victoria, and Dibombe (a defended post south-west of Jabassi).

French troops on the line of the Midland Railway up to and including Edea, which place was partially isolated as one span of the first of the two bridges had been destroyed. A detachment at Kribi was protecting that seaport from land attack.

Ships and armed craft of the Allied Navies had visited the whole of the Cameroons seaboard, and had established bases for small craft to patrol the rivers where navigable.

By this time approximately 1,000 male Europeans, only 32 of whom were incapable of bearing arms, had been deported for internment in Europe.

Towards the end of 1914 the French, under General Aymerich, and Belgian troops based on French Equatorial Africa, commenced to make their presence felt in the South and South-East, but my force was separated from them by a distance of approximately 400 miles.

In the North an Allied force was fully occupied in observing Mora and Garua.

At and near Ossidinge a small British force from Nigeria and German forces were in contact.

Notwithstanding the number of troops—British, French, and Belgian—in the country it was impossible at this period to co-ordinate their movements, owing to the vastness of the area over which they were scattered and the impossibility of establishing any means of intercommunication between the various Commanders. Furthermore, it was difficult for me to pursue a very active policy, as it was necessary to maintain comparatively strong garrisons in the places already occupied. Posts on our lines of communications were also absorbing troops from my somewhat depleted force, amongst which sickness was beginning to play its part.

7. It was on the 5th January that the German commander endeavoured to deliver a serious blow to the French force commanded by Colonel Mayer. Two practically simultaneous attacks were made against his force; the first at Kopongo, on the railway, the second at Edea, I had obtained some knowledge of the German commander's intention, and the post at Kopongo had been slightly augmented, with the happy result that the attack on this point was easily repulsed, but not until the railway and telegraph lines had both been cut and all communication with Edea severed. The troops at Edea had, however, to bear the brunt of a more serious movement.

The locality of Edea is by no means easy to defend owing to the proximity of the forest, the scattered nature of the buildings, and inequality of the ground; but so skilfully were the defences devised, and so good was the French marksmanship, that at the termination of the combat the Germans left on the field 23 Europeans dead and 190 native soldiers killed and wounded. The French loss consisted of 1 European sergeant and 3 *tirailleurs* killed and 11 *tirailleurs* wounded. A machine gun, number of rifles, ammunition and equipment fell into the French hands. It is significant that this was the first and last occasion on which the Germans attempted an operation of this nature on a comparatively large scale.

Towards the end of January, Lieut.-Colonel (now Brigadier-General) Cunliffe arrived at Duala on a mission from Lagos, and as a result of a conference it was agreed that a more active prosecution of the campaign in the Northern Cameroons should be undertaken. I detached Major (now Lieut.-Colonel) W. D. Wright, V.C, a most able officer, from the staff of the British Contingent under my command and placed his services at the disposal of the Officer Commanding the Allied Forces at Garua. I also arranged with Captain Fuller, R.N., for the despatch of a naval field gun to Yola, *via* the Niger and Benue Rivers, for eventual use against the forts at Garua.

The early days of February were marked by great hostile activity in the neighbourhood of Northern Railhead. Lieut. Colonel Cockburn, commanding a battalion of the Nigeria Regiment, had a serious encounter with the enemy at Mbureku on the morning of the 3rd February, resulting in the capture of the hostile camp, a large quantity of small-arm ammunition, and equipment. We were, however, unable to reap the full advantage of our success, as Lieut.-Colonel Cockburn was obliged to transfer his force to the neighbourhood of Harmann's Farm, where the Sierra Leone Battalion was engaged with the enemy. During these two incidents we lost nearly 120 native soldiers killed, wounded, or missing; but, after we had consolidated our position at Baré, the enemy did not follow up the slight advantage he had gained.

Constant activity during February had failed to gain for us any material advantage to the north of the railway, and there were a series of small incidents which culminated in the second attack by our troops on the points known as Stoebel's and Harmann's Farms on 4th March. I regret that this attack was not successful and we lost some valuable lives, including Major (Lieut.-Colonel) G. P. Newstead, commanding the Sierra Leone Battalion, and Captain C. H. Dinnen, Staff Captain, an officer of great promise. The enemy must, however, have suffered in a similar degree, as it was later found that he had evacuated his defensive position and retired further north.

During February I received valuable reinforcements from French and British West African Colonies, and I was enabled to reconstitute my force and place a more homogeneous unit at the disposal of Lieut. -Colonel R. A. de B. Rose, commanding the Gold Coast Regiment.

8. On the 12th March a mission from French Equatorial Africa, at the head of which was Monsieur Fourneau, Lieutenant-Gouverneur du Moyen Congo, reached Duala. Its object was to invite my co-operation in an immediate advance, in conjunction with the troops under General Aymerich from south-east and east, against Jaunde. Since the occupation of Duala, Jaunde had been transformed into the temporary seat of the Colonial Administration. I fully realised the political and strategic importance of Jaunde, but demurred embarking on such an operation at that moment. It was late in the season and the rains were already beginning, besides which the troops I was able to employ were insufficient to ensure success in the absence of effective co-operation, in the immediate vicinity of Jaunde, by the troops under General Aymerich.

Owing to the difficulty of communication it was quite unsafe to count on this. However, in view of the great advantage which would follow an early occupation of Jaunde, I consented to co-operate with all my available strength, and the 20th April was fixed as the date on which an advance should be made from the line Ngwe-So Dibanga, on the Kele River. I consequently entrained a British force, commanded by Lieut.-Colonel Haywood, on 7th April, which was to commence a methodical advance in co-operation with the French troops under Colonel Mayer. The forcing of the line of the Kele River and the position at Ngwe, both of which places were obstinately defended, occasioned my troops some losses. I further found it necessary to despatch a force to Sakbajeme to deny the crossing of the Sanaga River at that place to the enemy. It soon became evident that the enemy was withdrawing troops from other and more distant parts of the Colony to resist our further advance.

At midnight 23rd/24th April the blockade of the Cameroons was declared, and every artifice was used to deceive the enemy, and incessant and unremitting activity was maintained by the Royal Navy on the coast line, so as to induce the enemy to believe that disembarkation would be made at a point from which a force could be marched on Jaunde. Campo had been occupied by a naval detachment, and boat patrol of the river as far as Dipikar was maintained.

The advance from the line already mentioned was subsequently postponed till 1st May, on which date the French and British columns moved forward to make good Eseka and Wum Biagas respectively.

The French advance on Eseka was conducted with some difficulty, as broken bridges denied them the use of the railway line for supply trains. Commandant Mechet, who conducted the advance, successfully overcame all difficulties, and after being seriously opposed at Sende, reached Eseka on 11th May.

Turning to the British advance, on 1st May Lieut.-Colonel Haywood recommenced his march eastwards from Ngwe, and driving in the hostile outposts at Ndupe, on the 3rd May his force was facing the formidable position which the enemy had established on the left bank of the Mbila River at Wum Biagas. We captured the position on 4th May, but not without serious losses in European officers. A warm tribute is due to the bravery and steadiness displayed by our Native troops, and to the pluck and endurance of the European ranks in face of such stubborn resistance.

As previously arranged, the French force at Eseka now moved north and joined the British at Wum Biagas, and Colonel Mayer left Edea to assume command of the Allied expedition. Stores and supplies were pushed forward by road, and a naval 12-pounder gun was despatched to reinforce our artillery.

Owing to the heavy casualties which had occurred in the ranks of the two battalions of the Nigeria Regiment and the inability of Nigeria, owing to the many calls made by General Cunliffe's troops, to supply me with trained soldiers, I decided towards the end of May to establish a training depot at Duala. The recruits were enlisted in Nigeria, and transferred to Duala for training. This proved a great success, and by its means 536 soldiers were trained and passed into the ranks.

9. On 11th May I received a message from the Governor-General of French Equatorial Africa, which informed me that the progress of the troops under General Aymerich had not been as rapid as expected, and that as neither Dume nor Lomie had been captured, no definite date could be given for the advance from those places. As I realised that the advance on Jaunde, if delayed for any length of time, would be seriously interfered with by the rains, and the sickness among both Europeans and natives, which was already causing me some anxiety, would rapidly increase, I instructed Colonel Mayer to push on with all vigour, in consequence of which he left Wum Biagas on 25th May.

I regret that supply difficulties soon made themselves evident; the country was barren, and with all available carriers and the few motor vehicles at my disposal, at that time only three, I was unable to transport food for Europeans and natives with sufficient rapidity. Handicapped by the almost impenetrable bush and a terrain which afforded many defensive positions, the advance became exceedingly slow. At every turn of the road the advance was met by machine-gun fire, so that during the 25th and 26th May only 5 miles was made good.

It took two days to force the enemy from Njok. The enemy evidently had received reinforcements and commenced to interfere with our line of communication, which was peculiarly susceptible to attack, while the long convoys of carriers were singularly prone to panic. I received an appeal from Colonel Mayer for reinforcements, as in addition to other disabilities dysentery had broken out in his force. I sent forward such troops as were available and took measures to obtain more carriers from the West African Colonies.

From 31st May till 4th June Colonel Mayer was held up at a position at Matem which presented more than usual difficulties owing to the swamps, which rendered a turning movement impossible. By the 5th June only 12 miles from Wum Biagas had been made good. About this date Colonel Mayer informed me that owing to sickness, especially amongst Europeans, and to the stubborn resistance of the enemy, he was of opinion that the further advance of his column on Jaunde was impracticable, and he proposed, pending further instructions, to establish himself on the Puge River, where he could await the approach of General Aymerich's troops.

I immediately informed the Governor-General of Equatorial Africa of the situation, adding that unless he had recent news of General Aymerich's advance I should be obliged to withdraw Colonel Mayer's force to the line of the Kele River. On 7th June Governor-General Merlin informed me by telegraph that he had received no further news from the Southern Cameroons. I thereupon decided to withdraw our force to the Ndupe River preparatory to holding a line So Dibanga-Ngwe. A serious attack on one of our convoys of 500 carriers, and the consequent loss of food supplies, decided Colonel Mayer to retire without further delay.

During the 16th and 17th June our rear-guards were harassed, but never broken, and the enemy suffered considerably in his attacks. I deemed it advisable to send forward a reinforcement of the last troops at my disposal so that the pressure on our withdrawal could be relieved; these troops, after leaving Duala on the morning of the 15th June, bivouacked the following day at Ngui, 35 miles beyond Edea, having completed much of the distance in heavy tropical rains. On the following morning, after resuming their march, they reached Colonel Mayer's column at a most opportune moment during a heavy attack on the rear-guard. Not till 28th June did the hostile activity cease, when our posts were firmly established at Ngwe and on the Kele River at So Dibanga.

In comparison to the size of our force the casualties were serious, 25 *per cent*, being either killed or wounded. I regret that this operation was not more fruitful in results, and I fully recognise the fact that Colonel Mayer was not in a position to undertake, single-handed, an advance on Jaunde, but I had hoped that the pressure that was being brought on the hostile forces in the Southern Cameroons would have had the effect of preventing a concentration against us.

During this period our troops near Northern Railhead were not in a position to undertake any serious offensive action.

10. There was now an unavoidable lull in the operations caused by the rains. I seized this opportunity to send as many British officers and non-commissioned officers as possible to the United Kingdom for a

few weeks' rest, and I arranged that most of the native troops from Nigeria and the Gold Coast should, in turn, visit their own Colonies. I managed, however, to send detachments to operate near the Njong and Campo Rivers respectively. A French detachment from Ngwe also carried out a successful reconnaissance in July.

It was on 25th and 26th August 1915, at a conference which took place at Duala between Governor-General Merlin, General Aymerich, and myself, that the plan was decided on by which the Cameroons was eventually conquered.

The fall of Garua, in the north, early in June enabled a British and French force to be set free which could move through the highlands of the Cameroons to the south.

General Aymerich, whose troops were now established at Bertua and Dume, promised definite co-operation, with Jaunde, as before, the objective, whilst a force under Lieut.-Colonel le Meillour moved parallel to the eastern frontier of Muni, and was to cross the Campo River and move in the direction of Ebolowa. It was also arranged that I should show such activity as was possible from Northern Railhead so as to assist the British force at Ossidinge in its attempt to link up with other troops from Nigeria, and further that a force should land at Campo and move parallel to the northern frontier of Spanish Guinea.

It was unfortunate that Brigadier-General Cunliffe was unable to attend this conference, but all details were communicated to him, and he was asked to exercise all possible pressure from the north. His role was most admirably carried out.

The arrival of the 5th Light Infantry of the Indian Army strengthened my command, and further reinforcements from French West Africa were promised. The General Officer Commanding at Freetown and the Governors of Nigeria and the Gold Coast agreed to send me the carriers I required and to maintain them by monthly drafts. It was thanks to these officers that, in spite of a rather heavy sick roll among carriers, an efficient transport service was maintained throughout. My requirements in motor transport were also met; this service proved invaluable and far exceeded my expectations.

Thus, by 22nd September preparations were sufficiently far advanced for a move to be made in an easterly direction Many of the earlier operations were a repetition of those which had taken place in May and June, but the general plan differed in so much that I arranged for the British and French lines of supply to be kept distinct, whilst I also determined that Eseka should be made the French advanced base from which operations could be carried forward to the Jaunde-Kribi road, and that our general advance should be carried out by means of parallel columns by road and railway. Our communications needed much repair, including the total reconstruction of a heavy railway bridge and a deviation necessitating considerable labour on earthwork. Many other smaller bridges were broken or destroyed; those on the road were made fit for heavy traffic, those on the railway were practically rebuilt.

The British force, as previously, experienced stiff resistance at Wum Biagas, but on 9th October that place was captured after a lively action, in which the Nigerian and Gold Coast troops once more distinguished themselves. From here we were enabled to send out flanking columns and render some assistance to the French troops who were fighting their way to Eseka. The Kele River, in flood, proved a formidable obstacle, and its crossing somewhat delayed the British flanking columns sent out from Wum Biagas. Sende was occupied by the French on 25th October, and the enemy was driven from Eseka on 30th October.

Considerable rolling stock, left behind after our previous advance, was retaken, and proved a valuable addition to our exiguous supply of engines and wagons. By 23rd November, both British and French forces were ready for the final advance, the bush track from Edea to Wum Biagas had been converted into a good motor road, and through railway communication, Duala-Eseka, was nearing completion. There were also over 7,000 carriers employed on such sections of the communications as were still unfit for motor or rail traffic. Dschang Mangas was selected as the primary objective of the British force, whilst the French were directed to make good the line of the Jaunde-Kribi road. Both forces slightly modified their tactics, and the advance was generally carried out by a main body, with two wings moving on as wide a front as the nature of the country permitted. The method of our advance appears to have entirely disconcerted the enemy and, although he still continued strenuously to resist our advance, it became apparent that his strength was gradually becoming exhausted.

Towards the end of November, the fighting in and around Lesogs by the troops under Lieut. -Colonel Cockburn was of a very severe nature, but the troops from the Northern Provinces of Nigeria gallantly rose to the occasion and, despite all difficulties of the country, were not to be denied in their endeavour to dislodge the enemy. Much credit is due to these troops and their leaders for the admirable conduct of this operation. Ngung was reached on the 30th November, and, up to this place, every defensive position was disputed by the enemy. On 7th December the advance on Dschang Mangas was continued and both main and flank columns were subject to opposition. A well executed move by a small force of the Gold Coast Regiment, under Captain Butler, V.C., considerably disturbed the enemy; the capture of one of his machine guns and several thousand rounds of ammunition, in addition to important documents, produced considerable effect. On 17th December the more open and cultivated country was reached and we took Dschang Mangas.

From 26th November onwards, the French were fighting their way through very broken country to Mangeles; they had to face determined opposition and lost a considerable number of European and native soldiers, but their tenacity of purpose was rewarded by the capture of Mangeles on 21st December, after intermittent fighting covering a period of five days. The column halted at this place for rest and to establish a supply depot.

11. I must now indicate the turn that events had taken beyond Northern Railhead. I was informed from Nigeria that the British force at Ossidinge, under Major Crookenden, would be prepared to move on Bamenda on 12th October. I therefore ordered a force consisting of portions of the West African Regiment, 5th Light Infantry, and some artillery, under Lieut.-Colonel Cotton, 5th Light Infantry, to move on Dschang from Bare, also starting on 12th October. Hostile opposition was experienced at Mwu and Nkam Rivers and from an entrenched position at Sanschu. On 6th November Dschang was occupied.

On receipt of information that Major Crookenden's force had reached Bamenda on 22nd October I ordered Lieut.-Colonel Cotton to leave a garrison in Dschang and move a force to Bagam to co-operate with Major Crookenden in an attack on that place. The enemy had, however, forestalled us and withdrawn to Fumban, whither we pursued him after experiencing some difficulty in effecting the crossing of the Nun River. On 2nd December the important centre of Fumban was occupied and an abortive effort of the enemy to retake it was frustrated.

Brigadier-General Cunliffe, foreseeing the possibility of obstinate resistance at Fumban, had directed two other small columns to co-operate in our movement on that place. These columns arrived almost simultaneously with that under Lieut.-Colonel Cotton. Major Crook-enden's troops then continued their advance under Brigadier-General Cunliffe's direction, whilst I placed garrisons in Fumban, Bana, and Bagam, and the bulk of Lieut. Colonel Cotton's troops returned to railhead. I was thus enabled to withdraw a small force to move from Nkongsamba to Jabassi and penetrate the Bafia country, where I still believed there were small hostile parties. I also was enabled to detach a force to assist the French column operating from Campo.

I think I may consider our operations in the Northern area were entirely satisfactory, and the simultaneous advance of our columns took the heart out of the remnants of the enemy forces in that district. Furthermore, we had established touch with Brigadier-General Cunliffe's columns, which were now converging on the Sanaga River, at a point known as the Nachtigal Rapids. Our losses were slight and the health of all ranks was considerably better than that of the troops fighting in the lower altitudes.

12. Reverting to the operations of the main forces. On receiving information that the British force had arrived at Dschang Mangas, I decided that it would be more advantageous to move on Jaunde direct, rather than await the French advance to the Jaunde-Kribi road. In arriving at this decision, I was influenced by the fact that the mind of the native does not understand the meaning nor necessity of delay, and from a political point of view the early occupation of Jaunde appeared to be all important. From 22nd December, the hostile resistance gradually weakened, strongly entrenched positions were abandoned, and on the morning of the 1st January Colonel Gorges entered Jaunde with his force. The enemy appeared to have completely broken under the pressure which he was now experiencing from all sides.

Allied troops from the north, troops from French Equatorial Africa and the Belgian Congo commenced to arrive in Jaunde during the first week in January. It is, I think, a remarkable feat that troops that had fought and marched for a period of seventeen months should have converged on their objective within a few days of one another.

The direct effect of the occupation of Jaunde was to relieve all pressure in front of the French force advancing from Mangeles, the Jaunde-Kribi road being reached early in January. British and French forces were moved during the first week in January to Widemenge and in the direction of Ebolowa *via* Olama and Onana Besa crossings of the Njong River. At Kol Maka, Lieut.-Colonel Haywood succeeded in securing the release of officers, non-commissioned officers, civilian and native non-combatants who had been taken prisoners by the Germans at various times during the war; his force, supported by a strong French column, continued its advance on Ebolowa, on which place a second Allied column was also advancing.

A French force under Lieut.-Colonel Faucon occupied Ebolowa on 19th January, after experiencing some slight resistance. The definite move of the remnants of the German forces towards Spanish territory now became apparent, and Lieut.-Colonel Haywood proceeded with all despatch to follow them up as far as Nkan, from which place I diverted him *via* Efulen on Kribi, in order to clear the western area of stragglers. A British force was also moved to Lolodorf.

Colonel Morisson took command of a strong French force, and, moving towards the Spanish frontier, succeeded in driving the German force in front of him across the Campo River into neutral territory. A similar operation was conducted by the French force which had operated from Campo, so that by the middle of February no Germans were left in the Cameroons, and the conquest of the country had been completed. . . .

C. M. Dobell,
Major-General,
Commanding the Allied Forces.

Appendix 3

Lieutenant-General Smuts's First Dispatch.

General Headquarters,
East Africa, 30th April 1916.

My Lord,

In accordance with your instructions, I assumed command of His Majesty's Forces in East Africa on the 12th February, and sailed from South Africa on that day.

I arrived at Mombasa on the 19th of February, and was met there by Major-General Tighe, who explained to me fully the situation in East Africa and the steps he had taken to push forward all preparations for an operation in the Kilimanjaro area before the rains. I decided to visit immediately the two proposed lines of advance by Mbuyuni and Longido, and to make a personal reconnaissance in company with General Tighe.

★★★★★★

The East African dispatches include, besides the two of General Smuts's here printed, one from Lord Buxton, the High Commissioner of South Africa, describing the operations of the Rhodesian force and the Tanganyika Naval Expedition; one from General Northey, continuing the narrative to the beginning of 1917; one from General Hoskins, covering the period between January and May 1917; and one from General Van Deventer, describing the operations between May and November 1917, after he had taken over the command from General Hoskins.

★★★★★★

As a result of this reconnaissance I cabled your Lordship, on arrival at my General Headquarters in Nairobi on 23rd February, that I was

179

prepared to carry out the occupation of the Kilimanjaro area before the rainy season, and received your sanction on 25th February.

2. It will, I think, assist a clear understanding of this Dispatch if I here briefly recapitulate the outstanding features of the military situation in East Africa, and also the steps recently taken by General Tighe towards the development of the advance into German territory which was made possible by the arrival of the reinforcements from South Africa.

At the commencement of 1916 the German forces in German East Africa were estimated at some 16,000 men, of whom 2,000 were white, with 60 guns and 80 machine guns. They were organised in companies varying from 150 to 200 strong, with 10 *per cent*, of whites and an average of two machine guns per company.

The enemy occupied a considerable tract of British territory. At Taveta they had established a large entrenched camp, with an advanced position at Salaita (El Oldorobo), an entrenched camp at Serengeti, and an outpost at Mbuyuni, the latter places thirteen and seventeen miles respectively east of Taveta. At Kasigau they maintained a garrison of 500600 rifles, with the object of delaying our concentration by blowing up the Uganda railway and the Voi-Maktau railway. Their numerous attempts to accomplish this end were uniformly futile.

In the coastal area they maintained a considerable garrison on the Umba River, and actively patrolled thence to the vicinity of the Uganda railway, Mwele Mdogo, and Gazi. At numerous points throughout the 600 miles of land frontier the opposing troops were in touch, and the result was that General Tighe had to disseminate widely his small force, and was unable to keep any large reserve in hand to meet a sudden call.

GENERAL TIGHE'S GOOD WORK

In spite of the fact that he had to be constantly on the watch for the next move of his active and enterprising foe, General Tighe kept steadily before him the necessity of doing all in his power to prepare the way for the eventual offensive movement. With this end in view he organised such of his infantry as could be spared for active operations into the 1st and 2nd East African Brigades, acting on the Taveta and Longido lines respectively, and proceeded to develop the organisation of the whole force into two divisions and line of communication troops.

3. On the 15th January the 1st Division, under Major-General Stewart, was ordered to occupy Longido, and to develop the lines of communication between that place and Kajiado, on the Magadi railway. On the 22nd January the 2nd Division, under Brigadier-General Malleson, advanced from Maktau to Mbuyuni, meeting with slight opposition, and on the 24th occupied Serengeti camp. This advance had the immediate effect of making the enemy evacuate Kasigau. The railway was advanced from Maktau to Njoro drift, three miles east of Salaita, and arrangements made for the concentration of a large force at and near Mbuyuni.

The greatest difficulty in the way of this concentration was the lack of water, the Serengeti plains being by nature a waterless desert. A 2½-inch pipe was laid from Bura, but this did not suffice, over 100,000 gallons being required daily, and the pipe yielding only 40,000. The balance had to be made good by railway and storage tanks. The whole of the watering arrangements were so carefully worked out that not a single hitch occurred when the main concentration eventually took place, in spite of the fact that an enemy raiding party succeeded in damaging the Bura headworks. For this great credit is due to Lieutenant-Colonel C. B. Collins, R.E., who was General Tighe's C.R.E.

I cannot speak too highly of all the preliminary work done by General Tighe in the direction of organisation and preparation for offensive measures. This left me free on arrival to devote my whole energies to active operations, and I take this opportunity of placing on record my appreciation of the fact that the success of those operations is in a large measure due to General Tighe's foresight and energy in paving the way for the expected reinforcements.

4. Early in February the 2nd South African Infantry Brigade arrived, and on the 12th of that month General Tighe directed the 2nd Division to make a reconnaissance in force of Salaita, and if possible to occupy that position. General Malleson carried out this operation with three battalions 2nd South African Brigade and three battalions 1st East African Brigade, supported by 18 guns and howitzers. The Salaita position is one of considerable natural strength, and had been carefully entrenched. The enemy was found to be in force, and counter-attacked vigorously. General Malleson was compelled to withdraw to Serengeti; but much useful information had been gained, and the South African Infantry had learned some invaluable lessons in bush fighting, and also had opportunity to estimate the fighting qualities of their enemy.

5. This brings the operations up to the date on which I arrived in East Africa, and decided, as mentioned above, that the occupation of the Kilimanjaro area before the rainy season was a feasible operation.

The original plan devised by General Tighe had been to occupy the Kilimanjaro area by making a converging advance from Longido and Mbuyuni with the 1st and 2nd Divisions respectively, with Kahe as the point towards which movement was to be directed. To this main plan I adhered, but I decided that some alteration of dispositions was necessary in order to avoid frontal attacks against entrenched positions of the enemy in the dense bush, and to secure the rapidity of advance which appeared to me essential to the success of the operation in the short time at our disposal before the commencement of the rains, which might be expected towards the end of March.

Accordingly, I issued orders that the 1st South African Mounted Brigade, under the command of Brigadier-General Van Deventer, should be transferred from the 1st Division to Mbuyuni and act from there directly under my orders in a turning movement to the north of Taveta and Salaita. This transfer was carried out by rail most expeditiously, and by 4th March all minor concentrations were complete, the 3rd S.A. Brigade had arrived in the country, and my force was disposed as follows:—

1st Division (less 1st South African Mounted Brigade), Longido.

2nd Division (less detachments), Mbuyuni and Serengeti.

1st South African Mounted Brigade, Mbuyuni.

Army Artillery, Mbuyuni and Serengeti.

The 2nd South African Infantry Brigade, one field and one howitzer battery, were retained by me as Force Reserve.

PLANS FOR THE ADVANCE.

6. The general outline of my plan has been explained to your Lordship in various telegrams, but I will recapitulate the main points here.

The task of the 1st Division was to cross the 35 miles of waterless bush which lay between Longido and the Engare Nanjuki River, occupy the latter, and then advance between Meru and Kilimanjaro to Boma Jangombe. My intention was thereafter to direct this division on Kahe, and cut the enemy's line of communication by the Usambara Railway.

The task of the 1st South African Mounted Brigade and of the 2nd

Division was to advance through the gap between Kilimanjaro and the Pare Hills against the enemy's main force, which was reported to be concentrated in the neighbourhood of Taveta, with strong detachments at the head of Lake Jipe, in the bush east of the river Lumi and at Salaita. The total force with which the enemy could oppose our advance into the Kilimanjaro area was estimated at 6,000 rifles, with 37 machine guns and 16 guns.

7. The manner in which I proposed to initiate the operation was as follows:—

(a) 1st Division to commence its forward movement on the 5th March, and be allowed two clear days' start before the advance against Taveta should begin.

(b) 1st South African Mounted Brigade and 3rd South African Infantry Brigade, both under command of General Van Deventer, to leave Mbuyuni and Serengeti on the evening of the 7th March, and make a night march to the river Lumi east of Lake Chala. On the 8th to seize the high ground round Lake Chala and develop a turning movement by the west against Taveta. The object of this turning movement was partly to surprise the enemy and partly to avoid a frontal attack through the thick bush which lay between Salaita and Taveta.

(c) 2nd Division to advance against Salaita Hill on the morning of the 8th March, entrench a line facing the hill, and make preparations for an attack, supported by the Army Artillery.

(d) Force Reserve to follow General Van Deventer's column during the night of the 7th-8th March and take up a central position astride the Lumi, whence it could be used to reinforce either Van Deventer or the 2nd Division, as required.

It will be readily seen that these movements demanded the greatest energy and decision on the part of the commanders concerned. In order to be in close touch with the main operations round Taveta, I decided to accompany the Force Reserve to the Lumi, leaving part of my General Staff at Mbuyuni to control operations elsewhere.

The initial movements were carried out successfully and with very slight opposition on the part of the enemy, who was undoubtedly taken by surprise. The 1st Division succeeded in crossing the waterless belt safely, and by the afternoon of the 6th March had its advanced

183

troops established on the small hill Nagasseni just east of the river Engare Nanjuki. By 2 p.m. on the 7th the whole division was concentrated at this point, and on the 8th moved to Geraragua.

8. On the evening of the 7th March General Van Deventer's column started on its march across the Serengeti plains for Chala, the 1st South African Mounted Brigade from Mbuyuni, and the 3rd South African Infantry Brigade from Serengeti Camp. The Force Reserve, under General Beves, followed in rear of the 3rd South African Infantry Brigade.

At 6 a.m. on the 8th March the 1st South African Mounted Brigade reached the Lumi River near the southern end of the Ziwani swamp, and the 3rd South African Infantry Brigade simultaneously arrived on the river east of Lake Chala. General Van Deventer at once proceeded to make good the high ground lying between Lake Chala and Rombo Mission. He then made a converging movement on the Chala position from the east and north-west, sending the brigade scouts to threaten the enemy's line of retreat to the south. Chala was only lightly held by the enemy, and these dispositions soon caused him to withdraw on Taveta. General Van Deventer occupied Chala and pursued towards Taveta, a portion of which position was occupied by the 2nd South African Horse. As, however, the enemy in Taveta were in considerable strength, General Van Deventer considered it wise to concentrate on the Chala position before dark.

Meanwhile the 3rd South African Infantry Brigade and the Force Reserve halted astride the Lumi to guard the crossing. During the afternoon an enemy force estimated at from 300 to 500, which had been cut off from the main body by our unexpected movement to Chala, advanced from the north along the line of the river in thick bush, and made more than one attack on the outposts of the infantry in bivouacs. These attacks were easily repulsed with loss to the enemy, but also caused most of the losses we sustained that day.

While the bulk of my forces were engaged in making good the Chala position and the Lumi crossing, the 2nd Division, under Major-General Tighe, carried out, on the 8th March, an artillery bombardment of Salaita; and the infantry of the 1st East African Brigade advanced and dug themselves in, in readiness for an attack on the 9th.

TAVETA SEIZED

9. At dawn on the 9th General Van Deventer sent his mounted troops to get astride the Moschi road west of Taveta, which place the

enemy evacuated in the course of the day. He also sent the 12th South African Infantry to make good Ndui Ya Warombo Hill and the Lumi bridge east of Taveta. The 2nd Division continued to bombard Salaita, and at 2 p.m. the infantry advanced to the attack, only to find that the bombardment, coupled with the turning movement *via* Chala, had compelled the enemy to evacuate, just in time to avoid two squadrons of the 4th South African Horse sent to intercept their retreat.

10. Early on the 10th a regiment of South African Horse dispatched from Chala to make good Taveta were able to seize the position before a large body of the enemy, who had obviously been sent back to reoccupy it. After a brief fight the enemy withdrew towards the Latema-Reata *nek*, hotly pursued by mounted troops and field artillery. The enemy fought a stubborn rear-guard action, and eventually was left in position on the *nek*.

On the same date the 2nd Division advanced to Taveta, detaching garrisons at Serengeti and Salaita. The Lumi crossing was found impassable for motor lorries and heavy guns, and the bulk of the transport did not cross until the bridge had been improved about mid-day on the 11th.

11. On the morning of the 11th General Van Deventer on the right advanced *via* Spitze Hill and Kile on Mamba Mission and the line of the Himo. In the centre the 4th South African Horse, supported by the 12th South African Infantry, made good East Kitowo Hill after a brisk skirmish. On the left the mounted troops of the 2nd Division reconnoitred the Latema-Reata *nek*, which was found to be held in some strength. The Force Reserve was ordered to move from Chala to Taveta.

It was now clear that the enemy had withdrawn from Taveta in two directions—along the Taveta-Moschi road towards the west, and along the Taveta-Kahe road between Reata and Latema Hills towards the south-west; but the exact line of retirement of his main forces was uncertain.

The 4th S.A. Horse were in touch with what appeared to be merely a rear-guard on the Moschi road, and an enemy force of unknown strength was in position on the Latema-Reata *nek*. It was essential to determine whether this was only a covering force, or whether the enemy was in such strength as to threaten a counter-attack towards Taveta. In either case it was necessary to drive him from the *nek* before I could advance beyond Taveta.

The 2nd Division had in Taveta only three weak battalions of the 1st East African Brigade, eight 12 pr. guns and a howitzer battery. With these I determined to clear up the situation, and, if possible, make good the *nek*.

12. This operation was entrusted to Brigadier-General Malleson, commanding the 1st East African Brigade, who had at his disposal:

Belfield's Scouts.
Mounted Infantry Company.
Nos. 6 and 8 Field Batteries.
No. 134 Howitzer Battery.
2nd Rhodesian Regiment.
130th Baluchis.
3rd King's African Rifles.
Machine Gun Battery, Loyal North Lancs.
Volunteer Machine Gun Company.

General Malleson selected as his objective the spur of Latema, which commands the *nek* from the north, and at 11.45 a.m. advanced to the attack. The 130th Baluchis on the right and 3rd K.A.R. on the left formed the firing line, 2nd Rhodesian Regiment the general reserve. The mounted troops watched both flanks, and the artillery supported the attack at a range of about 3,500 yards.

As they approached the bush-clad slopes of Latema the firing line came under a heavy rifle and machine-gun fire. The enemy also had at least two guns and several pom-poms in action, and our infantry could make little headway.

13. At 4 p.m. the Force Reserve began to arrive in Taveta, and I reinforced the 2nd Division with the 5th South African Battalion. At the same time General Malleson, who was seriously indisposed, asked to be relieved of his command, and I directed General Tighe to assume command of the operation personally.

RHODESIANS' GALLANTRY.

On the arrival of the 5th South African Infantry, General Tighe ordered the Rhodesians to advance, and to carry the King's African Rifles forward with them in an assault on the Latema ridge, the 130th Baluchis co-operating vigorously on the right. All ground gained was to be at once made good. The 9th Field Battery and 5th South African

Field Battery, as they arrived in Taveta, were brought into action in support of the attack. This assault was gallantly pressed home, especially by the Rhodesians, but failed to make good the ridge. The 3rd K.A.R., who had been hotly engaged since the outset, had the misfortune to lose their gallant leader, Lieutenant-Colonel B. R. Graham, and several other officers. General Tighe found it necessary to support the Baluchis with half the 5th South African Infantry, and I further reinforced the 2nd Division with the 7th South African Infantry.

14. This latter battalion reached General Tighe about 8 p.m., and shortly afterwards he decided that the best chance of quickly dislodging the enemy from their position on the *nek* was to send in the two South African Battalions with the bayonet by night. This operation was no doubt fraught with considerable risk, as there was no opportunity of adequately reconnoitring the ground over which the attack must be made, nor was it by any means certain that the enemy was not present in large numbers. On the other hand, the moon was in the first quarter, and so facilitated movement up to midnight; the bush along the line of the road to the *nek* did not appear to be very dense; and, moreover, the volume of fire developed by the enemy did not seem to indicate that he had a large force actually in his first line, though he had, as usual, a large proportion of machine guns in action.

15. The night advance of the two South African Battalions was ably organised and gallantly led by Lieutenant-Colonel Byron, Commanding 5th South African Infantry. The 7th South African Infantry formed the 1st line, with the 5th in support. They advanced with great dash through the bush, which proved to be much thicker than was anticipated, driving the enemy before them till the latter was on the crest, where he checked our advance. A certain amount of disintegration was inevitable in a night advance through the dense thorn bush in the face of stubborn opposition. Groups of men and individuals who got separated from their leaders had no course but to fall back to the position where the 1st East African Brigade was formed up in general reserve, about 1,500 yards east of the *nek*.

NIGHT FIGHT IN THE BUSH.

Colonel Byron had issued instructions that, on reaching the crest, Lieutenant-Colonel Freeth, commanding the 7th South African Infantry, and Major Thompson, of the same battalion, should wheel outwards and make good the heights north and south of the *nek* respectively, while Colonel Byron himself secured the actual *nek*. These two gallant officers most ably carried out their task. Colonel Freeth fought his way up the steep spurs of Latema till he found that the party with him had dwindled to 18 men. He was joined by a few of the Rhodesians and King's African Rifles, who had clung on to the crest of the ridge after the assault in the evening, and the small party held on till daylight.

Major Thompson wheeled towards Reata with 170 men and dug himself in in an advantageous position. About midnight Colonel Byron reached the *nek* within 30 yards of the enemy's main position. The opposition here was very stubborn. At one point Major Mainprise, R.E., Brigade Major, and 22 men were killed by the concentrated fire of three machine guns; and Colonel Byron, who was himself slightly wounded, reached the *nek* with only 20 men. The enemy was still in a position which commanded the ground he had won, and finding it impossible either to advance or to hold his ground, he was reluctantly compelled to withdraw.

16. Meanwhile General Tighe found it extremely difficult to keep touch with the progress of the fight, of which he could only judge by the firing and the reports of officers and others sent back from the ridge, who naturally were only cognizant of events in their own immediate vicinity. About 1 a.m. several requests for reinforcements reached him, and he ordered forward the 130th Baluchis. These advanced at 1.20 a.m., and shortly met Colonel Byron, who reported that he had ordered his small party to retire. General Tighe accordingly re-formed his force and dug in astride the road to await daylight. Attempts to gain touch with Colonel Freeth and Major Thompson failed.

Judging by General Tighe's reports, I considered that it was inadvisable to press the direct attack on the Latema–Reata *nek* further, and preferred to await the effect of the turning movement of the mounted troops, which was ordered for the next morning, and calculated to cause a speedy withdrawal of the enemy from this position. I accordingly, at 4.30 a.m., directed General Tighe to withdraw his whole force before daybreak to a line further back from the *nek*. This withdrawal was in progress when patrols sent to gain touch with the flank detachments on Reata and Latema found the latter in occupation of both hills and the enemy in full retreat from the *nek*. I at once dispatched the 8th South African Infantry to make good the ridge, and some artillery to shell the retiring enemy, who was now estimated to be between 1,500 and 2,000 in number. Effective pursuit through the dense tropical forest which stretched from Kitowo to Kahe was out of the question.

17. Our casualties in the engagement were about 270, which cannot be considered excessive in view of the important results gained. We captured, besides rifles and ammunition, a 6-cm. gun and three machine guns. Some 40 to 50 enemy dead were found on the position, and as they are always most careful to remove their dead and wounded, there can be no doubt that their casualties were severe. While this action was in progress on the Taveta-Kahe road, the 4th South African Horse and 12th South African Infantry kept up a brisk engagement with the enemy on the Taveta-Moschi road, where the enemy was found to be in strong force on the northern slopes of Latema and on North Kitovo Hill. At one point 20 of the enemy dead were found after the engagement.

18. With the end of this action the first phase of the battle for Kilimanjaro came to a conclusion. On the 12th March General Van Deventer continued his advance up to Mamba Mission and the Himo Bridge on the Taveta-Moschi road, in the face of slight opposition. The enemy in his retirement during the night and the early morning had destroyed all bridges on the road, and great difficulty was experienced in rationing Van Deventer's force. On the 13th he advanced and occupied Moschi unopposed, the enemy having withdrawn the previous night towards Kahe. The 2nd and 3rd South African Brigades were thereupon concentrated at the Himo Bridge, the remainder of the 2nd Division at Taveta.

GENERAL STEWART'S FLANKING MOVEMENT.

19. It is necessary now to refer to the movements of the 1st Division, which had arrived at Geraragua on the 8th, having encountered only slight opposition. On the 9th General Stewart halted to reconnoitre and let his supplies catch up. The direct road from Geraragua to Boma-Ja-Ngombe was reported impassable for wheels, all bridges having been destroyed by the enemy. As a result of this and of the exhausted state of his ox transport, General Stewart considered it necessary to halt on the morning of the 10th, and reconnoitre for a road further to the west. A difficult but passable track was found, and the march was resumed at mid-day. The mounted troops left Geraragua at

16 hours on the 10th, on which date they encountered some opposition, sustaining 13 casualties.

The division and the mounted troops eventually joined hands on the Sanja River on the night of the 12th-13th, and on the 13th advanced to Boma-Ja-Ngombe. On the 14th, when the main force of the enemy had already retired to the Ruwu and Kahe positions, the 1st Division joined hands with General Van Deventer in New Moschi, through which place the six companies of the enemy who had been opposing General Stewart had already passed on the night of the 12th March, as previously stated.

20. The next few days, from the 13th to the 18th March, were spent in improving the road from Taveta to Moschi, reorganising transport, bringing up supplies, etc., and in reconnoitring towards Kahe and the Ruwu River. The whole of the country bordering that river on the north is dense tropical forest, and the enemy took advantage of this to display some boldness in firing into our camps by night.

On the night of the 17th-18th Belfield's Scouts were sent from Himo bridge to occupy Unterer Himo, and at dawn were driven off by a superior force of the enemy. A position on the Ruwu River appeared to me from patrols, intelligence reports, and somewhat incomplete air reconnaissance, to be the next which the enemy might hold, and it was of vital importance for purposes of railway extension and future advance that the enemy should be driven south of this river before the rains commenced.

I therefore, on the 18th, issued orders for a general advance towards the Ruwu. On the extreme right the East African Mounted Rifles and a squadron of the 17th Cavalry advanced from Mue *via* Masai Kraal. The 3rd South African Brigade moved from Himo bridge on Euphorbien Hill, and the 2nd South African Brigade from the same point on Unterer Himo, to which place the 1st East African Brigade of the 2nd Division sent forward two battalions from Latema. The advance was supported by field and mountain artillery. The infantry occupied the line Euphorbien Hill-Unterer Himo without difficulty, while the East African Mounted Rifles encountered three enemy companies at Masai Kraal. During the day I ordered the 2nd East African Brigade of the 1st Division from New Moschi to Mue, to support the mounted troops on the Kane road.

The Fight for Kahe Hill.

21. On the 19th the general advance continued, but the 1st East

African, 2nd and 3rd South African Brigades could make little progress through the well-nigh impenetrable bush which surrounded the enemy's position on the Himo about Rasthaus. The 3rd Brigade, ably supported by the 28th Mountain Battery, had a sharp engagement with the enemy at dusk while occupying its line for the night, and sustained 30-40 casualties. The fresh graves of twenty-seven of the enemy's *askaris* were afterwards found in the vicinity of the action. The 2nd East African Brigade and the mounted troops of the 1st Division under General Sheppard pushed the enemy back to Store, four miles south of Masai Kraal, and bivouacked there for the night.

On the 20th I withdrew the 2nd South African Brigade from Unterer Himo, and sent three battalions to reinforce General Sheppard on the Mue-Kahe Road, where I anticipated the strongest opposition. At 2 p.m. on the 20th General Van Deventer, with the 1st South African Mounted Brigade, the 4th South African Horse, and two field batteries, left Moschi with instructions to cross the Pangani, and get in rear of the enemy's position at Kahe Station. That night General Sheppard's camp at Store was heavily attacked from 9.30 p.m. to midnight. These attacks were repulsed with loss to the enemy. The enemy force actually engaged was estimated by prisoners at 500 men, with another 500 in reserve. Their casualties were estimated at 70-100, ours were 20.

22. At daylight on the 21st Van Deventer was approaching the Pangani from the west at a point south-west of Kahe Hill. He experienced some difficulty in crossing the river, but by mid-day had occupied in succession Kahe Hill, Bauman Hill, and Kahe Station with slight opposition. The enemy had already earlier in the day blown up the main railway bridge over the Ruwu (or Pangani).

After the loss of Kahe Hill the enemy realized its importance as the key to the Ruwu position, and made several determined attempts to recover it, which were, however, beaten back with loss. A mounted party which moved forward from Kahe Hill to cut off the retreat of the enemy by the wagon road south of the Ruwu found the enemy in force, and had to retire. Van Deventer therefore waited for the following day to develop the turning movement after his whole brigade should have been brought across the Pangani. During the whole day the enemy had two 4.1-inch naval guns in action, one on a railway truck and the other from a concealed fixed position south of the Ruwu.

23. On the 21st General Sheppard had the following troops under his command:—

2nd East African Brigade.
  25th Battalion, Royal Fusiliers.
  29th Punjabis.
  129th Baluchis.
2nd South African Brigade.
  5th South African Battalion.
  6th South African Battalion.
  8th South African Battalion
Divisional Troops.
  East African Mounted Rifles.
  1 Squadron 17th Cavalry.
  1st and 3rd South African Field Artillery Batteries.
  27th Mountain Battery.
  No. 12 Howitzer Battery.
  1st King's African Rifles.
  2 Royal Naval Armoured Cars.

As soon as I heard that General Van Deventer was nearing Kahe I ordered General Sheppard to advance. This he did at 11.30 a.m., with the 2nd South African Brigade on his right and the 2nd East African Brigade on his left, the dividing line being the Masai Kraal-Kahe road. By 12.30 p.m. the enemy had been driven back on to his main position on the south edge of a clearing in the dense bush, with his east and west flanks protected respectively by the Soko Nassai and the Defu Rivers, both of which were considerable obstacles to the movements of infantry. General Sheppard's intention was to attack the enemy frontally, and, with or without the aid of the 3rd South African Brigade, to envelop his right (eastern) flank.

"The Men Fought Like Heroes."

Unfortunately, the advance of the 3rd Brigade from Euphorbien Hill was so impeded by the dense bush that it was unable to exercise any influence on the fight, and without its aid the task proved to be beyond the powers of the force at General Sheppard's disposal. His infantry tried to cross the clearing, which varied in width from 600 to 1,200 yards; but the enemy's dispositions were so skilfully made that these attempts were met and repulsed by rifle and machine-gun fire, both from front and flank. Two double companies of the 129th Baluchis crossed the Soko Nassai, and endeavoured to turn the enemy's right; but here, too, they were held up. Our guns were well handled, the 27th Mountain Battery being in action in the actual firing line; but definite targets were difficult to obtain owing to the density of the bush. The whole force, in fact, was ably handled by General Sheppard; and the men fought like heroes, but they were unable to turn the enemy from his strong position.

General Sheppard did not know that Van Deventer was already at Kahe Station, some miles in advance of his right flank, and no contact could be established through the intervening thick bush. He accordingly gave orders to dig in on the ground won, with a view to renewing the attack on the 22nd. At dawn on the 22nd patrols found the enemy gone. He had waited only for the cover of night to retire across the Ruwu River, and proceed down the main road towards Lembeni, abandoning his stationary 4.1-inch gun, which had been blown up.

Our casualties at the Soko Nassai action were 288. It is not easy to estimate those of the enemy, but a large pile of used field-dressings found south of the Ruwu told a significant tale. As far as can be ascertained, the enemy forces employed on the 22nd were 14 or 15 companies, distributed along the Himo and Ruwu from Rasthaus to Kahe.

Besides the two 4.1-inch naval guns, the enemy employed several field guns and pom-poms.

24. The result of these operations from the 18th to 21st March was to drive the enemy out of the country north of and along the Ruwu River. Aruscha had meanwhile been occupied by our mounted scouts, who drove off an enemy company in a southerly direction, and thus the conquest of the Kilimanjaro Meru Area, probably the richest and most desirable district of German East Africa, was satisfactorily completed. I accordingly established my Headquarters at Moschi, placed a chain of outposts along the line of the Ruwu, and set to work to reorganise my force for the next move, meanwhile concentrating the troops as far as possible in healthy localities, to give the men a rest after the hardships they had endured.

SERVICES OF OFFICERS.

25. I am particularly indebted to the following officers for their services during the operations:—

Major-General M. J. Tighe, C.B., CLE., D.S.O., commanding the 2nd Division, loyally co-operated by carrying out my wishes in the spirit and the letter. He also commanded at the successful action at

Latema *nek*. I have already mentioned his great services in paving the way for the offensive campaign.

Brigadier-General J. L. Van Deventer, commanding 1st South African Mounted Brigade, commanded throughout the operations an independent column, and executed the turning movements to which the rapidity of our success was undoubtedly due. He displayed soldierly qualities of a high order in controlling the mounted troops in their long night marches and manoeuvres through unknown and extremely difficult country.

The Air Services performed valuable reconnaissance work throughout the operations, and on several occasions considerably demoralized the enemy by the use of bombs.

The Royal Artillery were ably handled by Brigadier-General J. H. V. Crowe, and on all occasions when they had an opportunity of preparing the way for and covering the infantry advance their support was most effective.

The Supply and Transport Services worked with great zeal, and the fact that no hitch occurred in the supply of units scattered over such a large area is evidence of the efficiency displayed by all executive ranks. Such roads as do exist are merely clearings through the bush and swamp, and these rapidly become well-nigh impassable for heavy lorries. The existing track had constantly to be improved, and deviations cut, causing endless delays, and the result was that transport drivers were frequently at work continuously night and day.

The rapidity of the advance, and the distance to which it was carried, must almost inevitably have caused a breakdown in the transport had it not been for the unremitting exertions of the railway engineers who carried forward the railway from the Njoro drift, east of Salaita, to Taveta and the Latema *nek* at an average rate of a mile a day, including surveying, heavy bush cutting, and the bridging of the Lumi River. This fine performance is largely due to the ripe experience and organising power of Colonel Sir W. Johns, Kt., CLE.

Exceptionally heavy work, too, has been thrown upon medical officers and personnel. All wounded have been treated and evacuated expeditiously, and the number of sick who passed daily through the hands of the medical authorities, more especially since the cessation of active operations, has been very great. Great credit is due to Surgeon-General G. D. Hunter, C.M.G., D.S.O., and his assistants.

The excellent manner in which communication has been maintained throughout reflects great credit on my Signal Service, the officers and men of which, under the able control of Lieutenant-Colonel H. C. Hawtrey, R.E., have spared no efforts in overcoming the many difficulties attendant on operating in such country and on such a large front.

The Officers of my Staff have throughout rendered me every possible assistance. I would especially mention Colonel (now Brigadier-General) J. J. Collyer, my chief of the General Staff, whose sound judgment, ability, and tact made possible the harmonious working of a curiously heterogeneous force; and Brigadier-General R. H. Ewart, C.B., CLE., D.S.O., A.D.C, Administrative Staff, who has done everything possible to perfect and co-ordinate the working of the various administrative services on which an army operating in equatorial Africa is peculiarly dependent.

Brigadier-General W. F. S. Edwards, D.S.O., my Inspector-General of Communications, rendered invaluable services, and the rapidity and smoothness with which the concentration of troops was carried out were very largely due to his energy and powers of organisation, while the manner in which he extended the lines of communication during the actual operations left nothing to be desired.

It is not easy for me to express my appreciation of the conduct of the troops during these operations. General and Staff Officers, Commanding, Regimental, and Departmental Officers, rank and file, and followers, British, South African, Indian, and African, all have worked with a zeal and single-minded devotion to duty that is beyond praise. Shortage of transport necessitated the force moving on light scale, and the majority of the troops had no more than a waterproof sheet and a blanket for three weeks on end. Rations at times unavoidably ran short. Long marches in the hot sun and occasional drenching rains were calculated to try the most hardened campaigner. Yet all these hardships were endured with unfailing cheerfulness, and a chance of dealing a blow at the enemy seemed to be the only recompense required.

A list of those officers and N.C.O.'s and men whom I desire to bring to your Lordship's special notice in connection with these operations will be forwarded at an early date.

I have the honour to be.

My Lord,

Your Lordship's obedient Servant,

J. C. Smuts, Lieutenant-General,
Commander-in-Chief, East African Force.

Appendix 4

Lieutenant-General Smuts's Second Dispatch.

General Headquarters,
East Africa, 27th October 1916.

Sir,

In my last Dispatch I described the brief but important operations which ended on 21st March in the occupation of the Kilimanjaro-Aruscha area.

The strategy involved in those operations was determined for me by the military situation I found existing on my arrival in British East Africa in February. The opposing armies had massed on the Taveta and Longido fronts; the rainy season was expected in a few weeks, and there was no time or necessity for radical alteration in the plans on which my predecessor had been working. When the operations came to an end it was necessary without delay to dispose my forces most advantageously with a view to their health and comfort during the approaching rainy season, and it became necessary to study the important question of the strategy to be followed in the future operations.

REORGANISATION OF FORCES.

(2) Preliminary to both matters, however, was the question of re-organisation of the East African forces, which I deemed necessary not only for the vigorous prosecution of the coming campaign, but also to secure the smooth and harmonious working of a most heterogeneous army, drawn from almost all continents and speaking a babel of languages. I decided to abolish the two Divisions formed by my predecessor and to organise my forces into three Divisions, two of which were to consist of the contingents from the Union of South Africa, and the third was to include the Indian and other British forces.

The Union Divisions were again so organised that each should eventually contain a mounted and an infantry brigade, so as to secure the necessary mobility to enable us to cope more expeditiously with the enemy *askari* army of fleet-footed Africans. In these alterations, as well as in all other important matters which I have had from time to time to submit for the sanction of the War Office, I have found the uniform and prompt support of the latter, for which I cannot be sufficiently grateful, and to which the success achieved in this campaign was in no small measure due. At the end of March, then, the East African Force—apart from lines of communication troops, under Brigadier-General W. F. S. Edwards, D.S.O., as I.G.C.—was organised as follows:—

The First Division, under Major-General A. R. Hoskins, C.M.G., D.S.O., comprised the First East African Brigade, under Brigadier-General S. H. Sheppard, D.S.O., and the Second East African Brigade, under Brigadier-General J. A. Hannyngton, C.M.G., D.S.O.

The Second Division, under Major-General J. L. Van Deventer, comprised the First South African Mounted Brigade, under Brigadier-General Manie Botha, and the Third South African Infantry Brigade, under Brigadier-General C. A. L. Berrange, C.M.G.

The Third Division, under Major-General Coen Brits, comprised the Second South African Mounted Brigade, under Brigadier-General B. Enslin, and the Second South African Infantry Brigade, under Brigadier-General P. S. Beves.

The Second South African Mounted Brigade arrived in May, and was ready to take the field in the latter half of June.

Having completed the above reorganisation, I disposed the infantry units as far as possible at suitable points on high and dry ground at Moschi, Himo, and Mbuyuni, with only advance guards along the deadly malarial line of the Ruwu, facing the enemy forces in the Pare mountains.

The First Mounted Brigade was pushed on to the Aruscha area, which was reported to be most suitable for horses, and at the end of March the whole brigade had arrived there.

General Plan of Invasion.

(3) The most important problem for consideration was the strategy to be followed in the coming campaign. As a result of the preceding operations we had just barely entered the enemy territory, which stretched out before us in enormous extent, with no known vital point

anywhere, containing no important cities or centres, with practically no roads, the only dominant economical features of the whole being the two railway systems. Faulty strategy at the beginning, a wrong line of invasion once entered upon, might lead to months of futile marching and wasted effort. All our information credited the enemy with the twofold intention of conducting an obstinate and prolonged campaign in the Pare and Usambara mountains, and thereafter retiring to fight out the last phases of the campaign in the Tabora area, from which much of his supplies and most of his recruits were drawn. Careful consideration was given to the various alternative lines of invasion that presented themselves.

(4) There was, in the first place, the possibility of advancing inland from the coast along the existing railway lines, which had been adopted with such signal success in the German South-West Africa campaign. An advance from Tanga was, however, ruled out because I considered the place of no importance after the Tanga railway had been reached further north. Much, on the other hand, was to be said for an advance inland from Dar-es-Salaam, the capture of which would have great political and military importance, and would much facilitate the transport and supply arrangements for the campaign into the interior. It was, however, also ruled out, partly because the prevalence of the south-east monsoon at that period makes a landing of a large force on that coast an operation of great difficulty and even danger, partly because a prolonged campaign on the coast immediately after the rainy season would mean the disappearance of a very large percentage of my army from malaria and other tropical ailments.

(5) In the second place, consideration was given to the question of an advance on Tabora by Victoria Nyanza, which we controlled, and Muanza, which would have to be wrested from the enemy. This plan had the advantage of presenting a comparatively short line of advance, and of promising to strike at the main recruiting ground of the enemy forces, as the German askaris would be loath to remain in the field after their homes and families had fallen into our hands. Its adoption, however, would involve the transfer to a distant theatre of a large part of our forces, while the enemy army would remain concentrated and ready to strike at our railway communications with the coast. But my main objection to adopting it was the consideration that to occupy so huge a territory as German East Africa within reasonable time a simultaneous advance from different points along different routes was essential.

Now in the Eastern Lake and Uganda area we already had a force of about 2,000 rifles; in addition, the Belgians had a very large force in the West, in the neighbourhood of Lake Kivu, with which they were prepared to invade the Ruanda and Urundi districts if we could assist them with the necessary transport and supply arrangements, *via* Victoria Nyanza. For the occupation of the Western parts of German East Africa it was therefore only necessary to make these arrangements, and thereby to set the Belgian and British forces simultaneously in sympathetic motion in the Ruanda and Bukoba districts respectively. This was done, and with the best results, as will be described later.

(6) There remained, then, the third and last alternative of either striking at the main enemy forces in the Pare and Usambara mountains along the Tanga railway line, or of launching an attack against the interior and the Central Railway from Aruscha. A movement against the enemy concentration along the Tanga railway had, however, several grave disadvantages. It was the step desired and expected by the enemy, as the massing of almost his entire fighting force in that area showed. It would involve a prolonged and costly campaign over terrain which nature and art had prepared admirably for defensive purposes. And at the end of such a campaign the entire enemy territory would still remain unoccupied, as the operations would have been conducted lengthwise all along the border.

On the other hand, an advance from Aruscha into the interior, if it was not to be a mere temporary raid but a secure and permanent occupation of the country, had to be in such force that it could meet any counter-attack by the enemy, who would in such counterattack have the advantage of his two railway systems, and so be practically moving on interior lines. Such an advance in force, therefore, ran the risk of weakening our forces in front of the enemy in the Pare and Usambara mountains, and of giving him an opening to attack our vulnerable communications both with the interior and the coast.

(7) In spite of these difficulties powerful arguments weighed with me in finally deciding in favour of an advance into the interior. I was informed that the violence of the coming rainy season would be mostly confined to the Kilimanjaro-Aruscha area; that farther West and South the rainy season was milder, and would not markedly interfere with military operations; and therefore, an advance into the interior would prevent our operations being brought to a complete standstill during the rainy months of April and May. In addition to this

the enemy had made the mistake of retiring south along the Tanga railway with practically his entire righting force, and the door to the interior stood wide open and unguarded.

Even the six companies which had operated between Kilimanjaro and Meru mountains against General Stewart's advance from Longido, and were expected by me to fall back on Aruscha and obstruct our advance in that direction, joined the enemy's main force at Kahe. A small detachment at Aruscha fell back before the advance of our mounted scouts, and when the mounted brigade arrived at Aruscha at the end of March, there was for the moment nothing to prevent an immediate movement into the heart of the enemy country. I decided to push the whole of the 2nd Division into the interior under Van Deventer, and for the present to keep the other two divisions with me in rain quarters, facing the enemy concentration south of the Ruwu.

In this way it would be possible to occupy a valuable portion of the enemy country within the next two months; and if, as I expected, this move would and must have the effect of compelling the enemy to withdraw large forces from the Pares and Usambaras to stem the tide of invasion into the interior, I could, if necessary, strengthen Van Deventer still further and yet have sufficient troops left to make a comparatively easy conquest of these mountains against the enemy's weakened defence. These anticipations were fully realised, as will be seen from the sequel.

Van Deventer's March to Kondoa Irangi.

(8) By 1st April the Headquarters of the 2nd Division, together with the 1st South African Mounted Brigade and two batteries of artillery, had reached Aruscha, while two battalions of the 3rd South African Infantry Brigade were on the way.

On the same day General Van Deventer reported that his scouts had engaged the enemy six miles north of Lolkissale, an isolated rocky hill in the Masai Steppe some 35 miles southwest of Aruscha. Further reports showed that this force consisted of a detachment of the enemy which had taken up a position covering the water springs on the hill, and that no other water was to be found in the vicinity. I therefore issued instructions that the movement southward should be initiated by the occupation of Lolkissale.

This operation was carried out with great skill by the 1st Mounted Brigade. On the morning of the 3rd April three regiments of South African Horse moved out from Aruscha, and during the night of

3rd~4th April surrounded Lolkissale. The enemy held the mountain with considerable determination, and fighting continued all day on the 4th and 5th; but at daybreak on the 6th the whole force, consisting of the 28th Field Company and Kaempfe's Detachment numbering 17 whites and 404 *askaris* with porters and two machine guns, surrendered. Our horses had been without water since noon of the 3rd. A large quantity of stores, ammunition, pack animals, etc., fell into our hands, while from information obtained from prisoners and captured documents it was ascertained that the enemy contemplated reinforcing Ufiome and Kondoa Irangi, and that the garrisons at these places had received instructions to hold out as long as possible. As it was evident that the bulk of these reinforcements must be sent from the troops on the Usambara Railway., and that several weeks must elapse before they could arrive, I decided to press forward the movement southwards of the 2nd Division as rapidly as possible, and ordered General Van Deventer to send his mounted troops to occupy Ufiome, Umbulu, and Kondoa Irangi before the enemy could reinforce them—the remainder of the 2nd Division to follow in support of the mounted troops.

(9) The 1st Mounted Brigade continued its advance to Ufiome on the 7th, encountering the enemy's patrols at various points of the route, and dispersing them with loss in killed and prisoners. On the 10th the enemy were located holding a *kopje* in the vicinity of Ufiome, and on the 11th the Brigade advanced from the Tarangire River. This movement resulted in the occupation of Ufiome on the 13th, the garrison of about 20 whites and 200 *askaris* retiring into the mountains, leaving 30 prisoners, some wounded, and a large quantity of supplies in our hands. The enemy was pursued for 20 miles south to Kisesse and Ssalanga, retiring in disorder.

(10) As the horses of the 1st Mounted Brigade were greatly exhausted by the continuous marching and fighting, a halt was made at Ssalanga until the 17th. The 4th South African Horse had in the meantime been sent by me to join the 2nd Division, and on its arrival, was directed on Umbugwe with instructions to clear Umbulu of the enemy.

The 10th South African Infantry and 28th Mountain Battery were also detailed by General Van Deventer to follow in support of the 4th South African Horse. Umbulu was finally occupied on 11th May, about one company of the enemy being driven out with loss.

The advance southward continued on the 17th, and contact was made with the enemy four miles north of Kondoa Irangi on the same day. Fighting continued till noon of the 19th, when our troops occupied Kondoa Irangi with no casualties, having inflicted a loss on the enemy of 20 killed, and 4 whites and 30 *askaris* captured. The enemy succeeded in destroying the wireless station and a portion of his supplies, but left behind about 80 rifles with much ammunition, and 800 head of cattle.

(11) General Van Deventer reported after this action that his horses were so exhausted that he would not be able to move until remounts arrived. He had lost hundreds of animals from horse sickness during his advance of some 200 miles from Moschi in the last four weeks, and his troops were worn out with ceaseless marching and fighting. I therefore decided that the 2nd Division should concentrate at Kondoa Irangi with detachments at Ufiome and Umbulu, and send patrols towards the Central Railway, Ssingida, Mkalama, and Handeni. During the remainder of the month and the first few days of May this concentration was gradually effected. The expedition, conducted by Van Deventer with his usual dash and resourcefulness, had secured important results at a trifling cost. Within a month of the battle of Kahe we had taken possession of the high, healthy, and fertile plateau which connects Aruscha with the Central Railway, and had occupied the dominant strategic points for any further advance, whether that was to be in the direction of the Central Railway, or westward to Tabora, or even eastward towards Handeni and the Eastern Usambara.

(12) Meanwhile, by the middle of April, the rainy season had set in with the greatest violence in the whole area from Taveta to Kondoa Irangi. The numerous rivers came down in flood, and swept away almost all our laboriously built bridges, the roads became impassable mud tracks, and all transport became a physical impossibility. The rains fell steadily day after day, sometimes as much as four inches in one day, and the low-lying parts of the country assumed the appearance of lakes. Fortunately, the railway had by this time reached Taveta, where sufficient supplies could be dumped for our resting troops.

The extension of the line was energetically continued to join the Kahe-Moschi railway, although for long distances the track was practically under water, and the attention of thousands of labourers was constantly required to prevent its disappearance in the mud. Van Deventer's Division in the interior was cut off, and managed to live for weeks on such supplies as could be collected locally, or could be carried by porters from Lolkissale for a distance of 120 miles. The strain and privation were, however, bound to be reflected in the general state of health of the troops.

(13) Meanwhile, also, the enemy had realized the tremendous threat which this expedition constituted against his whole scheme of defence, and, thanks to the onset of the rainy season bringing General Van Deventer's movement to a standstill, he was able to take measures to avert the danger to his rear by hurriedly transferring a great part of his force from the Usambara to the Central Railway, moving by rail to Mombo, thence by road to Morogoro or Kilossa, and again by rail to Dodoma.

This movement placed him in a position to concentrate some 4,000 men against the 2nd Division, which was at the time so weakened by sickness and unavoidable detachments that it could barely dispose of 3,000 rifles in its isolated position at Kondoa Irangi. The enemy, perceiving this, felt encouraged to assume the offensive, and advanced from the Central Railway in the early days of May, arriving on the 7th within six miles of Kondoa Irangi.

General Van Deventer gradually withdrew his advanced posts in face of this movement, keeping touch with the enemy, and finally disposed his force in defensive positions on a perimeter of about five miles frontage round Kondoa.

(14) On the 9th the enemy drove in our outlying piquets southeast of the village, and at 7.30 p.m. began an attack which lasted for nearly eight hours. This attack was pressed with determination, the enemy making four separate onslaughts, the brunt of which fell on the 11th South African Infantry, supported by the 12th South African Infantry. In some places the enemy repeatedly charged right up to our positions. Firing finally ceased at 3.15 a.m. on the 10th, when the enemy withdrew, leaving three whites and fifty-eight *askaris* dead on the ground, and five wounded as prisoners. There were numerous signs on the ground of further casualties. Our own losses were two officers and four other ranks killed, one officer and seventeen other ranks wounded. From information obtained as a result of the fighting it was found that the enemy had about twenty-five companies engaged, under the personal command of Colonel von Lettow, the German commander-in-chief. His force was organised as three battalions and one smaller detachment. One battalion commander, von Kornatzky,

was killed, and another, von Bock, wounded.

(15) With this defeat, the enemy's last hope of successful resistance to any large portion of our forces was extinguished. He continued in position round Kondoa during the remainder of May and the greater part of June, keeping for the most part to the thick bush, and engaging in desultory fighting and occasional long-range bombardment. General Van Deventer was unable to assume the offensive on any large scale on account of his weakness in horseflesh, the heavy sick rate amongst his men, and the great difficulties of supply over a line of communication of two hundred miles of quagmire; and had therefore to content himself with minor operations and enterprises while reorganising his forces and calling in his detachments from elsewhere. The 10th South African Infantry Regiment and 28th Mountain Battery arrived from Umbulu on 22nd May. I had already decided to strengthen the 2nd Division with two more battalions, the 7th and 8th South African Infantry Regiments, and additional artillery and machine guns, all from the 3rd Division, and these reinforcements eventually reached the Division on 23rd May and following days.

OCCUPATION OF THE PARE, USAMBARA, AND HANDENI AREAS.

(16) Such was the position when, towards the end of the second week in May, the rains abated, the ground once more began to harden, and it became evident that a general movement would soon again be possible. The direction of that movement was settled for me by the necessity of clearing the enemy from the Pare and Usambara mountains before the further invasion of German East Africa could safely proceed. The general conception was to move eastward along these mountains and at a point opposite Handeni to swing South and march towards the Central Railway in a movement parallel to that of Van Deventer.

The concentration of the enemy forces in front of Kondoa now made the occupation of the Pares and Usambaras comparatively easy, but the advance had to be rapidly executed to forestall any return movement of the enemy from Kondoa to the Handeni or Usambara area. Moving through the Masai Steppe along the old caravan route from Kondoa to Handeni, the enemy could reach the latter place in twelve days, and in two or three days more could be on the Tanga Railway at Korogwe. It was therefore advisable for my advance to reach the Western Usambara in a fortnight; further, if it could reach Handeni before the arrival of strong enemy reinforcements, I would have a second force almost the same distance from the Central Railway as that at Kondoa, and it would be impossible for the enemy to make effective resistance to the simultaneous advance of both columns situated 170 miles apart.

The nature of the country was, however, such as almost to preclude all rapidity of movement. The Pares and Usambaras are huge blocks of mountains with fertile valleys; the southern slopes are precipitous, and immediately below runs the Tanga railway, while further south dense bush extends for 17 to 20 miles to the Pangani, an impassable river flowing almost parallel to the railway and the mountains. The enemy held the mountains and the railway, and had outposts along the Pangani River.

Our advance was expected to follow the railway, which had been fortified at all convenient points for a hundred miles; and the enemy had therefore every reason to expect that the force opposing us, consisting of from 1,200 to 2,000 troops with field and naval guns, would render our progress sufficiently slow to enable him to send any necessary reinforcements. I therefore decided on the following dispositions for my advance. The main column, with most of the artillery and transport, was to proceed down the inner or left bank of the Pangani, somewhat in advance of another smaller column following the railway line, while a third small column was to start from Mbuyuni and enter the North Pares from the north side through the Ngulu Gap, joining the centre column at Same Pass between the middle and South Pares. In this way, with my flanks well forward in the mountains and along the Pangani, any real resistance of the enemy in his well-prepared positions in the centre along the railway would become hopeless. The advance commenced on 18th May by the movement of Lieutenant-Colonel T. O. Fitzgerald's battalion of the 3rd King's African Rifles from Mbuyuni to the Ngulu Gap, and on the 22nd May Brigadier-General Hannyngton's brigade moved from Ruwu along the railway, while Generals Sheppard's and Beves' brigades moved down the Pangani River accompanied by Major-General Hoskins and myself.

(17) The enemy's first position was reported to be at Lembeni, at which place the railway takes a sharp bend in towards the mountains and the ground is most suitable for defensive action.

I trusted, however, to turn this position either directly by Fitzgerald's column forcing its way through the Ngulu Gap, or indirectly by the continued advance of the Pangani column past the enemy's position.

The turning movements proved successful, and the enemy evacuated the Lembeni position on 24th May; on the following day Hannyngton occupied Same station without opposition, and on the 26th May Fitzgerald's column joined Hannyngton's and thereafter formed part of it. Hannyngton was ordered to proceed on the 28th over Same Pass along the road which passes through the South Pare mountain, and thence through the Gonja Gap between this mountain and the Usambara on to Mkomazi River. This move would prevent the enemy from making a stand on the railway along the South Pare mountain, and would at the same time clear the enemy out of the Gonja Gap. It was completely successful; on the 29th Hannyngton reached Gonja, and two days after the Mkomazi road bridge.

(18) Meanwhile the advance of the main column continued steadily along the Pangani, the advanced guards and mounted troops continuing to keep touch with the enemy's rear-guards, and I soon discovered that it was his intention to make his next stand near Mikotscheni, at which place the Pangani River rejoins the railway close to the mountains.

On the 29th May the advanced troops came up against this position and drew fire from a naval 4.1-inch gun and two field guns. On the 30th May the 2nd Rhodesian Regiment attacked the position in front, while the rest of General Sheppard's brigade made an arduous but successful turning movement by our left. The enemy retired in the night along the railway, leaving part of a new bridge in process of construction behind him. Buiko station was occupied by us the following day.

(19) Leaving a rear-guard of two companies in front of Hannyngton at Mkomazi, the enemy's main body retired along the railway to Mombo station, whence a trolley line proceeds to Handeni. They then followed this trolley line and entrenched themselves at Mkalamo where this line crosses the Pangani River. This retirement made it clear that the enemy was not going to make a stand in the Usambara, but intended to retire to Handeni and on to the Central Railway. I decided, therefore, to cross to the right bank of the Pangani with the main column, and to leave the further clearing of the Usambara district to Hannyngton. The rapidity of our advance had exceeded my best expectations. We had reached the Usambara in ten days, covering a distance of about 130 miles over trackless country along the Pangani River and through the mountains.

(20) As at this point a short pause in the operations was necessary to enable the German bridge over the Pangani to be completed, and to give the railway time to catch up with the advance, I proceeded on 2nd June *via* Moschi to Kondea Irangi, to visit the 2nd Division and to arrange personally the plans for future co-operation between my two widely separated forces.

On my return on 7th June I found that the German bridge over the Pangani had been completed and another smaller: one made close to Buiko railway station, roads had been cut through the bush, and another 30 miles south had been covered by the main column along the right bank of the Pangani.

(21) I had instructed General Hannyngton with his brigade to proceed down the railway line with Mombo as his objective. He advanced to Mazinde station on 8th June and occupied Mombo on 9th June, meeting with only slight opposition and capturing a machine gun from the enemy. The enemy retired south along the railway. On the same date the main force of the enemy was encountered by our main column entrenched at Mkalamo, and the 1st East African Brigade had a sharp action, lasting till nightfall. The enemy retired in the night, leaving numerous dead on the ground.

At Mkalamo the trolley line from Mombo to Handeni was reached on the 10th, and thereafter the advance to Handeni continued for a considerable distance along its route. The trolley line leaves the Pangani at Luchomo, and from that point proceeds in a southerly direction to Nderema, 2 miles west of Handeni. Between Luchomo and Nderema is a dry belt of 32 miles, the only water being found by digging in a dry river bed at Mbagui, 22 miles south of Luchomo. To cross this distance General Sheppard was sent forward with two battalions to press the enemy back until Mbagui was reached on the 13th. From there he worked forward to within five miles of Handeni, where the enemy was on 15th June found to hold a strongly entrenched position.

It was therefore decided to send Beves' brigade from Mbagui by a more westerly route through Gitu to Ssangeni on the Mssangassi River, 10 miles west of Handeni, where good water was found on the 17th June, and on the following day the brigade was launched against the enemy's southward line of retreat from Handeni at Pongwe and another point 4 miles north of Pongwe. At both places the enemy's retreating forces were beaten with heavy loss and driven into the bush, a pom-pom gun being subsequently found abandoned in the bush by the enemy. On the following day Handeni and Nderema were occupied by Sheppard.

On the same day Colonel J. J. Byron's battalion (5th South African Infantry) was sent in pursuit of the enemy to occupy Kangata, 8 miles south of Pongwe. They found the enemy in a concealed entrenched position in dense bush, and in the fight which ensued lost heavily, but held on staunchly until night, when the enemy retreated. At Kangata the main column for the first time since leaving Kahe came into a made road (the main road between Handeni and Morogoro), having marched for about 200 miles along routes prepared by themselves, mostly by cutting through the bush.

(22) During these operations General Hannyngton had occupied Wilhelmstal unopposed on the 12th June, and advanced along the Tanga railway as far as Korogwe on the 15th, where the wagon bridge had fortunately been saved by his special exertions.

From this point he was instructed to move along the Korogwe-Handeni road and to rejoin with all speed the 1st Division, which was now nearing Handeni. He reached Handeni on 20th June, the day after its occupation by Sheppard.

(23) The advance of the main column in pursuit of the enemy continued, and he was next reported as holding a strong position on the Lukigura River. I therefore divided my force in the hope of getting round his position with a flying column and compelling him to stand or fight.

General Hoskins with two South African Infantry battalions, a composite battalion of Kashmir Imperial Service Infantry, 25th Royal Fusiliers, and a small body of mounted Scouts, marched on the night of 23rd June to a point on the Lukigura River, north of the bridge held by the enemy. This force crossed the river the next morning, and then got astride the road behind the enemy's position. The remainder of the 1st Division under command of General Sheppard advanced direct on the enemy's position.

At midday on 24th June both columns engaged the enemy on three sides, and after some resistance defeated him, with a loss of 7 whites killed and wounded, 14 white prisoners, 30 *askaris* killed and many wounded and captured, together with the capture of two machine guns and parts of a third, one pom-pom and much ammunition. The Fusiliers and Kashmiris specially distinguished themselves in this action, in which only the dense bush enabled the enemy force to escape from complete capture.

(24) We had now reached the eastern slopes of the Nguru block of mountains, and immediately in our front was the high Kanga mountain. There was every indication that the enemy was massing in great force in both mountains in front of us, as well as on our right flank, and that any further movement would have to slow down. Our transport had reached the utmost radius of its capacity, and the troops had been on half rations for some time. They also required rest and reorganisation. Several units were reduced to 30 *per cent,* of their original effectives, owing to the ravages of malaria, and the difficulties of evacuating the sick were as great as those of forwarding supplies and reinforcements.

Since 22nd May the troops had marched considerably over 200 miles in difficult country, often having to cut their way through almost impenetrable bush, and constantly engaging the enemy in his prepared rear-guard positions. The march was rendered more arduous by most serious transport and supply difficulties, and, for the last 80 miles since leaving the Pangani, frequent shortage of water for both men and animals. Besides, I deemed it necessary, in view of the ever growing supply difficulties, to repair and restore the Mombo-Nderema trolley line before moving further.

Further, it was necessary for the execution of my plans that the 2nd Division should be more advanced before the combined movement against the enemy's main forces on the Central Railway should begin.

I therefore formed a large standing camp on the Msiha River, some 8 miles beyond the Lukigura, in which to rest and refit the troops prior to the next phase of operations.

Occupation of Coastal Area to Bagamoyo.

(25) The pause on the Msiha River enabled me also to deal with another matter which was rapidly becoming urgent. I had deliberately left the East Usambara area alone while pushing the enemy forces in front of me back as fast and as far as possible. The situation on my left flank towards the sea would either clear itself up by the retirement of the small enemy forces in that area, or, if necessary, they could be dealt with at a more convenient time. The railway line beyond Korogwe and the lower reaches of the Pangani River were, therefore, for the present left unoccupied. Steps were, however, taken to seize Tanga.

On 16th June the 5th Indian Infantry, moving south towards the border, occupied Mwakijembe, which the enemy had held strongly for a long time as a base from which to raid and bomb the Mombasa railway. The enemy force of about one company retreated towards the coast north of Tanga. Arrangements were then made by the Inspector-General of Communications for the landing of a force under Colonel C. U. Price, C.M.G., at Kwale Bay, 8 miles north of Tanga, and a simultaneous attack on that port by land and sea. This force, after slight opposition, arrived before Tanga on the 7th July simultaneously with the navy, and occupied it practically without opposition.

The enemy, consisting of two companies, was expected to retire towards Pangani, but did not do so, and continued to hang about in the vicinity, and on several occasions even indulged in some sniping into the town. At the same time the small force of about two companies which had retired before Hannyngton from Korogwe along the Pangani, returned and showed signs of aggressiveness. Small raiding parties kept interfering with our telegraph line, and convoys between Korogwe and Handeni, and finally, early on the morning of the 13th July, a determined attack was made on the road bridge at Korogwe, which was, however, successfully beaten back.

(26) The time had come to secure my rear and left from this guerilla warfare. Accordingly I ordered the Inspector-General of Communications, General Edwards, to make the following dispositions:—
To send part of the 5th Indian Infantry from Tanga along the railway to Muhesa; to send the 57th Rifles from Korogwe along the railway also to Muhesa, with a small detachment on their left in the direction of Amani; from Muhesa the 57th Rifles to proceed to the coast at Pangani, which was to be seized in co-operation with the navy. In the meantime, another detachment, under Lieutenant-Colonel C. W. Wilkinson, consisting of Railway Sappers and Miners, Jhind Imperial Service Infantry, and other details, was to proceed from Korogwe down the Pangani River to deal with the enemy force which had attacked the bridge, and which was reported to be at Segera Hill some distance down the right bank of the Pangani.

All these movements were duly and successfully executed. At Amani about 25 enemy whites surrendered without opposition. Colonel Wilkinson surprised and defeated the enemy at Segera Hill at dawn on the 15th July, and captured from them a Hotchkiss gun in good order, with ammunition, and thereafter pursued the enemy south towards Hale and Kwa Mugwe (Hoffman's plantation). The 57th, after reaching Muhesa, proceeded to Pangani, which had been previously occupied by the navy on the 23rd July. In the meantime, as I thought an effort should be made to capture these enemy parties, I had directed General Hannyngton's brigade to return from Lukigura to Handeni, and from there to march along the old caravan route towards Pangani, so as to intercept the retreating enemy and to clear the country of all raiding parties.

He reached Ngambo about midway between Handeni and Pangani on the 21st July, but found the enemy had already slipped through, part proceeding to the coast at Mkwadja, and the greater part retiring south along a track which proceeds by Rugusi and Manga (about 40 miles south-east of Handeni), in a southerly direction towards Mandera, on the Wami River. Accordingly, I ordered General Hannyngton to send Lieutenant-Colonel W. J. Mitchell, with a detachment of the 40th Pathans, after the enemy on this route, and to return with the rest of his brigade, as well as the 57th Rifles, to Lukigura, which was reached in time for them to take part in the operations through the Nguru Mountains.

Colonel Mitchell, in the meantime, had overtaken the enemy at Manga, at the same time as a cooperating detachment of the Cape Corps, sent from Kangata; the enemy was beaten and driven south to Mandera. Sadani Bay was occupied by the navy on the 1st August, and a detachment of the West India Regiment was landed and moved south and then westward towards Mandera to cooperate with Mitchell in clearing the enemy from the lower Wami River. This was successfully carried out, and thereafter the combined force, marched south-east to Bagamoyo, which had been brilliantly occupied by the navy on the 15th August, with the capture of a 4.1-inch naval gun in good order with ammunition.

From Bagamoyo this force was to form part of a larger movement for the investment and capture of Dar-es-Salaam. The military operations on the coast and parallel to it were, subject to the I. G. C.'s orders, under the command of Colonel C. U. Price, C.M.G., and were ably carried out.

Operations in Western Lake Area.

(27) To gain a complete picture of the state of the campaign in the northern parts of German East Africa at the end of June it is desirable at this point to consider the operations which were in progress in the west in the neighbourhood of the Great Lakes.

During the months in which my main columns were operating in the Kilimanjaro, Kondoa and Usambara areas and pressing their advance to the Central Railway, the "Lake Detachment," consisting of the 98th Infantry, 4th Battalion King's African Rifles, Baganda Rifles, Nandi Scouts, and other small irregular units, had not remained inactive.

Previous to the inception of active operations in East Africa the task originally assigned to the detachment had been the defence of the Uganda and British East Africa frontiers on both sides of Lake Victoria, and this task had been faithfully carried out for many long months. Although no engagement of importance took place, there was constant activity, and minor affairs of posts and patrols on the 300 miles of front were of almost daily occurrence. This necessarily entailed a continued state of vigilance and strain and demanded a high state of efficiency on the part of all ranks. That this was maintained is amply shown by the success achieved whenever opportunity offered. An instance of this had occurred just before my arrival, when the small post of one officer and 35 men at Machumbe had utterly defeated a raid of the enemy, causing him a loss of 3 whites and 22 blacks killed and 1 white and 31 blacks captured.

Apart from the minor operations of the Lake Detachment, my principal concern in the west was to make the necessary arrangements to facilitate the advance of Major-General Tombeur's Belgian forces. As an advance from his headquarters at Kibati, north of Lake Kivu, over the barren region of active volcanoes and in face of strong German opposition was impracticable, an arrangement had been concluded whereby part of General Tombeur's force was to move northeast to Lutobo, in order to advance from there in a southerly direction against Kigali, the capital of the rich German province of Ruanda.

To enable him to do so it was also agreed that the base for this force should shift to Bukakata, on Lake Victoria, 150 miles further east, and that we should be responsible for the transport and supply arrangements from this base. Owing to a variety of causes, the organisation and execution of these transport and supply arrangements proved a matter of considerable difficulty; and in consequence I sent Brigadier-General the Hon. Sir Charles Crewe, K.C.M.G., C.B., of my staff, to the Lake area to keep in touch with General Tombeur, to advise me in regard to all necessary requirements, and to push the arrangements on as fast as possible.

All difficulties were eventually overcome by General Tombeur and my representatives, and towards the end of April the advanced Belgian column under Colonel Molitor arrived at Kamwezi, 10 miles southeast of Lutobo. Thereafter rapid progress was made, and Kigali was occupied on the 6th May. The occupation of Kigali made the position of the German forces further west on the Belgian border untenable, and enabled General Tombeur to push forward columns both from the north and the south of Lake Kivu. It also became possible for Colonel Molitor's column to resume the advance to the southern end of Lake Victoria, and on the 24th June the Kagera River was reached.

(28) As the Belgian advance towards Lake Victoria progressed during April, May and June, our troops further north on the Kagera line increased their activity against the enemy opposed to them, and began gradually to drive him from his advanced posts. This withdrawal enabled our forces to become more concentrated, and finally it was found possible to release sufficient troops for an operation against Ukerewe Island. This island, the largest in Lake Victoria, lies immediately to the north of the German port of Mwanza, and produces much of the rice which forms the staple diet of a large part of the enemy's native troops. The island is within a few hours of Mwanza, and forms a favourable base for an operation against that town.

The operation for its capture was skilfully carried out on 9th June by Lieutenant-Colonel D. R. Adye, commanding the Lake Detachment, in conjunction with the Naval Flotilla on the lake under Commander Thornley, R.N. The enemy was completely surprised, eight German whites, about 60; blacks, and two small field guns being captured.

(29) As the withdrawal of the enemy from the Northern Kagera River and Karagwe district became accelerated, it also became possible to concentrate our scattered posts in that area into a mobile fighting force which could act more effectively against the retreating enemy. For this purpose, Brigadier-General Sir Charles Crewe was appointed to the Lake command in the middle of June. With his mobile column he first occupied Bukoba and Karagwe districts, and then proceeded south to arrange a combined forward movement with the Belgian forces. The advanced parties of the Belgian column had in the meantime reached Namirembe, at the southwest corner of Lake Victoria, at the end of June, the main body further west being hotly engaged with the German forces retreating from the north.

Sir Charles Crewe came to the sound conclusion that the course which promised the best results was a movement of his force against the important fortified town of Mwanza, the occupation of which would give us an excellent base at the south of the Lake for the forward movement of the combined British and Belgian forces to Tabora. Accordingly, on the 9th, 10th, and 11th July, he embarked his force, consisting of about 1,800 rifles, at Namirembe and Ukerewe Island, and on the night of the nth landed a column under Lieutenant-Colonel C. R. Burgess at Kongoro Point, east of Mwanza, and the following day another column, under Lieutenant-Colonel H. B. Towse, further north at Senga Point.

By the skilful disposition and movement of both columns—the one from the east, the other from the north-east—on Mwanza, he made it impossible for the enemy to withstand his advance; and the threat to the enemy's retreat from Burgess' column made the enemy evacuate the town on the 14th July. Most of the whites escaped down the Gulf in the s.s. *Mwanza* and *Heinrich Otto* and the steam pinnace *Schwaben*, with some lighters and boats, while about 400 to 500 *askaris* escaped down the main Tabora road. The enemy destroyed the powerful wireless station, but left a 4.1-inch naval gun in our hands.

The pursuit was continued next day, both by a force moving down the Tabora road and by another embarked on the s.s. *Winifred*, which was disembarked some 22 miles south of Mwanza. Some distance south 5 German whites were captured, and the enemy steamers and lighters were found abandoned; much baggage and stores and ammunition, a Colt gun, and even much specie were found abandoned by the enemy in his headlong flight. The pursuit was continued as far south as Misungi, opposite the southern end of Stuhlmann's Sound. The s.s. *Mwanza* and the lighters have since been salved, and are now in active use. Our total losses in this operation were quite insignificant, while the enemy had been skilfully ousted from one of his most important strongholds. The rapidity with which the enemy abandoned his valuable Lake Provinces and Mwanza was a clear indication that the eventual retreat would not be towards Tabora, but further east towards Dar-es-Salaam, or south towards Mahenge.

Van Deventer's Advance to Central Railway.

(30) I now turn back to review the main operations further east, and shall begin with Van Deventer's advance to the Central Railway. On the 24th June the 1st and 3rd Divisions came to a halt at the foot of the Nguru mountains. On the same day Van Deventer, with the

2nd Division, attacked the enemy positions all along the line round Kondoa Irangi and succeeded in occupying them with comparatively small loss. For some time, information had been received to the effect that a considerable transference of enemy forces from Kondoa to the Nguru front was in progress, and the enemy at Kondoa had been displaying a certain nervous activity and aggressiveness which are often the prelude of preparations for a retirement.

After the action of the 24th June Van Deventer proceeded to collect sufficient transport and supplies for the forward movement to the Central Railway. My orders to him were to clear his right flank towards Ssingida, to move a small column along the Saranda road towards Kilimatinde, and to move his main force towards Dodoma and further east on the road to Mpapua. My object was not only the occupation of the Central Railway, but more especially the movement of Van Deventer's force to the east so as to get into closer co-operation with the force at the Nguru mountains in dealing with the main enemy forces as they fell back to the Central Railway.

Lieutenant-Colonel A. J. Taylor was on 26th July sent with one infantry battalion, one mounted squadron and an artillery section to Ssingida, which, after some skirmishing on the way, was occupied on the 2nd August. A post was left there, and the balance of the column marched south to Kilimatinde. A similar sized column, under Lieutenant-Colonel H. J. Kirkpatrick, was on 14th July sent direct towards Saranda. Little opposition was encountered until they reached Mpondi, about twenty-four miles north-east of Saranda station. Here, in a country covered with very dense bush where scouting was well-nigh impossible, they suddenly found themselves under heavy machine-gun fire from a well-prepared enemy position. There was no alternative but to go straight for the enemy in a frontal attack. The attack was successful, Mpondi was occupied the same afternoon, our losses being eight killed and nine wounded. The advance was continued next day, and on 31st July the Central Railway at Saranda was occupied, as well as Kilimatinde, seven miles further south.

(31) Van Deventer's main column, moving south along the Dodoma road, occupied Chamballa (Jambalo) unopposed on the 18th July and Aneti on the 19th July. The country further south was reported to be waterless and the enemy to be entrenched at the water-holes at Tissa Kwa Meda and Tschenene. Van Deventer therefore divided this force into two columns, and ordered General Manie Botha to

move the Mounted Brigade by Tissa Kwa Meda and Njangalo towards Kikombo station on the Central Railway, while General Berrange, with two infantry battalions, a motorcycle corps and mounted scouts, was ordered to move by Tschenene and Meia Meia towards Dodoma. On the 25th July Tschenene was occupied with small loss, notwithstanding the strong enemy entrenchments, the success being largely due to the excellent work of the Armoured Motor Battery, which engaged the enemy at close range. On the 27th July Meia Meia was occupied, and part of an enemy mounted detachment was captured without any loss to us. On the 29th July Berrange occupied the Central Railway at Dodoma.

In the meantime, the First Mounted Brigade had occupied Tissa Kwa Meda after a sharp engagement on the 22nd July. From here Brigadier-General Manie Botha, who had rendered great service at the head of this brigade, returned to the Union of South Africa on private business, and his place was taken by Brigadier-General A. H. M. Nussey, D.S.O., who had been Van Deventer's Chief Staff Officer. After occupying Naju and Membe the Mounted Brigade on the 28th July reached Njangalo, where the enemy was driven from a strong position with the loss of a machine gun and 1,500 head of cattle. Kikombo station was reached on 30th July.

(32) By the end of July, a hundred miles of the Central Railway was thus in our possession. Practically every bridge or culvert was found blown up, but our advance had been so rapid that the enemy had had no time for further destruction of the track. General Van Deventer spent the following week in concentrating his forces now scattered along the railway from Saranda to Kikombo, at Njangalo, which is on the main road to Mpapua.

In the meantime, serious attention was given to the transport and supply situation, which—already grave enough at Kondoa with a transport distance of 200 miles from the Moschi railhead—had now become still graver by the addition of more than a hundred miles, and for the immediate future presented the baffling problem of having to provide for another 120 miles in the advance to Kilossa. How this problem was solved, and Van Deventer's force could be supplied for the advance to Kilossa, and even beyond to the Great Ruaha River, will be explained later.

The concentration of his Division at Njangalo was completed on the 9th August, and the advance was resumed on that date. But the sequence of events requires me now to turn to the operations through the Nguru mountains.

ADVANCE THROUGH NGURU MOUNTAINS.

(33) The general situation in German East Africa in the first week of August may be summarised as follows:—

Van Deventer had occupied the Central Railway from Kilimatinde to Dodoma; in the Lake area the British and Belgian forces were well south of Lake Victoria and preparing for a combined move towards Tabora. Further west a Belgian force had crossed Lake Tanganyika and occupied Ujiji and Kigoma, the terminus of the Central Railway. In the south-west General Northey's force had occupied Malangali after a brilliant little action, and was prepared to move towards Iringa, seventy miles further north-east. All coast towns as far south as Sadani had been occupied, and a small column was working its way southward to the Wami River and clearing the country between the Nguru mountains and the coast. The time had therefore come for the First and Third Divisions to resume the advance to the Central Railway. Hannyngton's brigade had rejoined the First, and Enslin's Mounted Brigade had joined the Third Division at Lukigura.

(34) For a distance of about forty-five miles the main road to the Central Railway passes close under the Nguru and Kanga mountains. The enemy had skilfully disposed about twenty companies or 3,000 rifles, with much heavy and light artillery, in the mountains and athwart the main road, which had been entrenched along the numerous foothills which the road crosses. If we forced our way down the road against these formidable obstacles or moved by our left flank through the bush and tall elephant grass, part of the enemy force in the mountains on our right would get behind us and endanger our communications. It was therefore essential to advance by way of the mountains themselves and to clear them as the advance proceeded southward. This could best be done by wide turning movements through the mountains, which would have the effect of threatening or cutting off the enemy's retreat if he delayed his retirement unduly.

The main block of the Nguru mountains on the west is divided from the Kanga mountain and foothills of Nguru on the east by the rough valley of the Mdjonga River, which flows from Mahassi at the northern entrance to the mountains due south towards Turiani, where the main road round Kanga crosses it. Into this river two streams run from the northwest through gaps in the Nguru mountains, the one entering the valley near Matamondo, the other by Mhonda Mission Station, near Turiani. Along both these streams rough mountain footpaths pass to the track which follows the course of the Mdjonga River. The enemy held the Mdjonga valley strongly from Mahassi to Turiani, and a turning movement would have to be further west so as to close in either at Matamondo or Mhonda Mission.

My information was that both the Mdjonga track and the Mhonda footpaths were capable of carrying wheeled traffic. I therefore decided on the following dispositions for the advance. While General Sheppard's brigade was to make a feint from Msiha camp directly against the enemy's position at Ruhungu, on the main road, he was to move the bulk of his brigade by his left flank so as to arrive at Russongo River, six miles behind the Ruhungu entrenchments. General Hannyngton's brigade was previously to have moved to Mahassi, and from there, accompanied by General Hoskins, was to advance along and clear the Mdjonga valley. Brits' Division was at the same time to make a detour to the north by the Lukigura valley, and then, turning west through Kimbe, to enter the mountains further west of Mahassi and emerge from the mountains through the Mhonda gap behind the enemy's forces disposed along Kanga and the Mdjonga valley.

(35) On the 5th August General Enslin moved with the 2nd Mounted Brigade from Lukigura *via* Kimbe, and the following day entered the Nguru mountains some eight miles west of Mahassi. On the 6th Beves' Brigade followed the same route, while General Hannyngton marched along mountain footpaths straight from Lukigura to Mahassi. On the 7th General Sheppard moved out from Msiha camp. General Hannyngton worked his way down the Mdjonga valley and found no strong opposition until he reached Matamondo on the 9th. In the meantime, Enslin had been moving rapidly through the mountains, and had arrived in the Mhonda gap and proceeded to occupy Mhonda on the 8th. He sent back word that the route through the mountains was entirely impracticable for wheeled traffic of any description. In consequence all our transport was sent back to Lukigura to follow Sheppard along the main road.

Hoskins had also returned to rejoin Sheppard, and in view of the strong opposition Hannyngton was meeting at Matamondo and the impracticability of the mountains, I directed General Brits to take Beves' brigade down the footpath to Matamondo to reinforce Hannyngton. One of Enslin's mounted regiments had lost its way in the mountains, and had also finally emerged at Matamondo. With the balance of his brigade, Enslin passed through the Mhonda gap and seized a series of positions across the road by which the enemy had to retire. These, however, he found it impossible to hold in view of the smallness of his force and threatened enemy attacks on his flanks. He, however, maintained his position at Mhonda Mission, and thereby forced the enemy everywhere to abandon his defence in the mountains and retire as fast as he could. If the terrain had permitted of the original scheme being carried out, and the whole Third Division had proceeded to Mhonda, the retreat of the enemy from these mountains would probably have been impossible.

(36) After stubborn fighting at Matamondo on the 10th and 11th the enemy was driven south with great loss, and a machine gun was captured from him. Our loss amounted to about sixty killed and wounded. On the 11th General Sheppard had worked his way through the dense bush round the enemy positions on the slopes of Kanga and had arrived at the Russongo River only to find the enemy gone. On the 12th I directed him to proceed due south by Mafleta to the Wami River at Kipera so as to be well on the left flank of the retiring enemy; he reached Mafleta on the same day, and on the following day occupied Kipera, where a small enemy patrol was driven off and a light bridge over the Wami was saved.

On the 12th and 13th the other brigades had reached Turiani, the enemy having fallen back some miles further south. It was becoming clear that we were now dealing with only part of his force, and that the balance had retired further south towards the Central Railway, either in the direction of Morogoro or Kilossa. Our progress was, however, very much hampered by the numerous rivers flowing from the Kanga and Nguru mountains, over all of which the bridges had been destroyed and had to be rebuilt by us, including some of very considerable dimensions.

In spite of this and other difficulties I decided to give the enemy no time, and ordered Enslin's Mounted Brigade to proceed the same day (13th August) round the left flank along the Liwale River to Ngulu on the Mkindu River, where he was to be joined by the 130th Baluchis from Kipera, and thence to make for Kwedihombo and Mwomero, where the roads for Morogoro and Kilossa respectively leave the Nguru mountains. At the same time Hannyngton's brigade was to work its way south along the main road. On the 15th both these places were occupied by Enslin and Hannyngton after only slight opposition.

(37) The bulk of the enemy force retired along the Morogoro road towards Dakawa on the Wami River, while a few companies went off along the Kilossa road. General Hannyngton was ordered to Mwomero to follow the latter to the Mkundi River, while the rest of the force was ordered to follow the enemy to Dakawa. General Sheppard had been ordered to cross the Wami at Kipera and to move his brigade along the right or southern bank of the Wami to Dakawa crossing. Sheppard and Enslin arrived on opposite banks at the enemy position on the 16th August, but the enemy was strong enough to hold Sheppard at bay some two miles north and at the same time to prevent Enslin from attempting to cross the river, which is both wide and deep.

The mounted men got across the river higher up the following day, and the enemy retired precipitately as soon as he discovered the threat to his line of retreat. The Crossing was occupied by us the following morning (18th August). Our losses in this action amounted to about 120, while the enemy had been very severely handled. A halt ensued here, as the bridging of the river was estimated to take four days. During this time Hannyngton was ordered to move his brigade to Dakawa, and the Cape Corps to take its place in following the retreating enemy party towards Kilossa. This pause provides a suitable opportunity to review Van Deventer's operations along the Central Railway.

Van Deventer's Advance to Kilossa and Great Ruaha River.

(38) On 9th August Van Deventer's Division had been concentrated at Njangalo, while the enemy was reported holding Tschunjo Pass with his left on Gulwe and his right on Kongoa. The advance was commenced on that day, and contact was established with the enemy at Tschunjo on the afternoon of the nth.

The troops had to march from Njangalo to Tschunjo over a waterless area, and went into action without any rest. Fighting continued nearly all night, and next morning the enemy was found to have retired, and was immediately pursued towards Mpapua, where he was again engaged and defeated before nightfall on the same day (12th August). Fighting and marching had been continuous for forty-two miles. The enemy force from Tschunjo to Mpapua consisted of twelve companies supported by artillery. Owing to the difficulties of the country the flanking movements were delayed and the advance had to depend for progress mainly on frontal attacks.

On the 15th August the enemy was again engaged at Kidete station, holding a strong position. He was supported by machine, field and heavy guns. On the 16th August the engagement at Kidete was continued until late in the day. The enemy was driven out by a flanking movement by the mounted troops who attacked in rear. Our casualties were six killed and thirty-nine wounded.

From 15th August to 22nd August our troops were in daily contact with the enemy, driving him gradually from Kidete along the railway line to Kilossa and Kimamba, which were both entered on the 22nd August, the day before our advance was resumed on the Wami River.

(39) In reporting these arduous operations General Van Deventer says:—

The railway from Kidete to Kilossa for a distance of twenty-five miles follows a narrow defile cut through the Usugara mountains by the Mkondokwa River; every yard of advance was stubbornly resisted by the enemy. Of the more important engagements those on the 19th at Msagara and on the 21st before Kilossa should be mentioned. In all the actions on this advance the fighting consisted of the enemy receiving our advance guard with one or several ambushes, then falling back on a well-prepared position, and retiring from that on to further well-selected ambush places and positions. All the time our less advanced troops were subjected to vigorous shelling by means of long-range naval guns.

Since leaving Kondoa Irangi the troops who have reached Kilossa by the shortest route have done at least 220 miles. Those troops who have gone *via* Kilimatinde and other places have done many more miles. Owing to bad roads, shortage of transport and the rapidity of advance, the adequate rationing of the troops was not possible. The underfeeding and overworking are sadly reflected in their state of health. Regarding the animals of my division, the advance from Mpapua to Kilossa was through one continual fly belt, where practically all the animals were infected.

After the occupation of Kilossa it was ascertained that the enemy held Uleia, twenty miles south, in force, and was being reinforced by troops from the Southern Command, who had opposed General Northey's advance. As my division was now weakened by the absence of the First Mounted Brigade (less one regiment), which had gone to Mlali on 25th August to co-operate with the Second Mounted Brigade, and as my infantry was in an exhausted condition, the commander-in-chief's wire of 26th August, asking for an advance on Kidodi and Kidatu, imposed a task which I had not intended to ask from my troops before they had had some rest. The advance was, however, ordered in accordance with the request of the commander-in-chief, the enemy being driven out of Uleia on 26th August and out of Kidodi on 10th September.

From Uleia to Kidodi the country consists of high mountain ridges running across the road for several miles. These had all been entrenched by the enemy some time ago, so that in the various actions his troops could fall back from one entrenched position to the next, a mile or so in rear. The operations thus called for an extraordinary amount of mountain climbing and constant fighting.

The slight casualties sustained in the various engagements over an enormous track of country, bristling with *dongas* and difficulties at every point, were mainly due to the advance being carried out by avoiding as far as possible frontal attacks. Dispositions were made with a view to carry out flanking movements while holding the enemy to the position occupied by him, but this the enemy carefully avoided, and under cover of darkness the engagement was usually broken off and a retreat effected.

The success with which the whole movement from Kondoa Irangi to the Central Railway, thence to Kilossa, and on to the Ruaha River, was carried out is due to the loyal cooperation and splendid spirit displayed by all units under my command.

It is difficult to express my high appreciation of the conduct and spirit of the troops, who all worked with determination and zeal; their endurance and hardships during long marches through dry and waterless stretches on scanty rations form an achievement worthy of South African troops.

Occupation of Morogoro and of Uluguru Mountains.

(40) When the advance through the Nguru mountains began I entertained some hope that, even if we failed in cornering the enemy in those mountains, he might still be brought to bay at Kilossa, on the Central Railway. Our information tended strongly to show that, if the

enemy retired from the railway, Mahenge would be his next objective; and as the most convenient point of departure for Mahenge appeared to be Kilossa, there was some justification for the hope that our rapid advance from the north and west might cut the enemy off in the direction of Kilossa. It may, however, have been the rapid progress of Van Deventer towards Kilossa that caused the enemy to retire with his main force towards Morogoro. Whatever the cause, our information did not leave us in any doubt as to the fact that the bulk of the enemy forces had retired to Morogoro.

The next move now was to try and bring the enemy to bay at Morogoro, if possible. To this end Enslin, whose brigade had been ordered to the Central Railway on the 21st August and had occupied Mkata station on the 23rd August, was ordered to proceed immediately to Mlali, about fifteen miles south-west of Morogoro, on the road to Kissaka, round the west of the Uluguru mountains. Mlali was successfully occupied by him on the 24th August. General Van Deventer was asked to send the First Mounted Brigade, under General Nussey, to reinforce Enslin so that it would be impossible for the enemy to force his way south by that route. The next point was so to arrange the advance of our other forces from Dakawa as to block also the road leading from Morogoro by Kiroka, round the eastern slopes of the Uluguru mountains, and thus to bottle the enemy up in Morogoro.

I was not then aware that a track went due south from Morogoro through the mountains to Kissaki, and that the capture of the flanks of the mountains would not achieve the end in view. On the morning of the 23rd August our forces crossed the Wami by the now completed bridge, but instead of moving forward to Morogoro we moved backward down the right bank of the Wami for about nine miles, and from there struck due east so as to cross the waterless belt of about twenty-five miles to the Ngerengere River, north-east of Morogoro. Owing to the nature of the country and the bush, the heat, and the absence of water, the march for that and the following day proved one of the most trying of the whole campaign; but on the night of the 24th August we were encamped on the Ngerengere River, in the neighbourhood of Msungulu, some eighteen miles north-east of Morogoro.

A mounted detachment under Colonel A. Brink, General Brits' Chief Staff Officer, had preceded us, and had that morning seized Mkogwa Hill, some three miles further south-east on the other side of the river. The move must have been a surprise to the enemy, who, evidently misled by Enslin's march into the belief that the whole force would move to Morogoro by the west, had massed his forces on the road between Dakawa and Morogoro and further west along the railway. Owing to the exhaustion of man and beast, the next day was spent in reconnoitring the country, and on the 26th August the advance was resumed, General Hannyngton being directed to Mikesse station, twenty miles east of Morogoro, and the brigades of Sheppard and Beves moving up the Ngerengere towards Morogoro.

Both places were occupied on the 26th August, only, however, to find that the enemy had gone, the Commander-in-Chief von Lettow and Governor Schnee with a force on the track due south of Morogoro through the mountains, and another force by the eastern or Kiroka route, while Enslin was engaged with a third force at Mlali. At Morogoro I found many proofs of the precipitate flight and demoralized condition of the enemy forces, and I decided to continue the pursuit in spite of the fact that my forces and animals were worn out with the exertions of the last three weeks and that my transport had reached its extreme radius of action. General Sheppard occupied Kiroka on the 26th, and General Hannyngton was ordered to continue the advance south after the retreating enemy. By the 30th August the First Division had pressed the enemy over the Ruwu, having been continually engaged with him since the 27th.

(41) It is unnecessary to describe in detail the events of our advance along the eastern slopes of the Uluguru mountains. The enemy fought rear-guard actions every day, and I held up our advance at every convenient place. Unfortunately, the country is very well suited to his tactics. The road passes through very difficult broken foothills, covered either with bush or grass growing from six to twelve feet high, through which any progress was slow, painful and dangerous. The bridging of the Ruwu took several days, and for some distance beyond the road passes along the face of precipitous rocks, round which the enemy had constructed a gallery on piles to afford a track for his transport.

As the gallery would not carry our mechanical transport, it took us some days to blast away the mountain side and construct a proper road. The gallery would not carry the 4.1-inch naval gun of the enemy, which was found destroyed near the Ruwu. South of the Ruwu, towards the Mwuna River, our advance proceeded not only along the main road to Tulo, but also on a track to the west of it to Kassanga, and to the east of it by the Tununguo Mission Station. The nature of the country and the continual fighting made our daily progress slow, while road-making and bridging behind engaged the attention, not only of the pioneers, but of a large portion of the troops as well.

Between the Ruwu and Mwuha Rivers the road passes first through swampy country and then over one of the spurs of the Uluguru mountains, which ends with a precipitous face, to the south. Through this spur and down this face a mountain pass was cut in the rock, which took the technical corps, as well as most of General Sheppard's brigade, several weeks, and will remain a notable and enduring engineering feat. Almost every day prisoners were taken, and in one of these daily actions a machine gun was captured. On the 10th September Tulo was occupied, and Hannyngton's brigade, which was leading the advance, moved on towards Dutumi, where the enemy made a resolute stand for several days, being only finally driven south to the Mgeta River on the 13th September.

(42) I now turn back to review the operations inside and along the western slopes of the Uluguru mountains. As already stated, General Enslin's Mounted Brigade reached Mlali on the 24th August from Mkata station. Early on the morning of that day the advance scouts of the brigade rushed Kisagale Hill, a small isolated hill athwart the road to the south, and captured an ammunition depot of the enemy, in which about one thousand shells for the naval and other guns of the enemy were found. At the same time one of the regiments galloped up the valley to the north of this hill, just as an enemy force was coming down the Morogoro road, and took up positions in the foothills in the immediate neighbourhood.

In the afternoon this regiment, after severe fighting, found their positions in the valley untenable, as the enemy was gradually working round them in the hills and bringing converging fire to bear on them. They retired a short distance to the south, but remained in possession of the road. Fighting continued during the following day, and as the enemy found it impossible to dislodge our men from the road, they destroyed two naval guns, one 3.4-inch and the other 4.1-inch, and retired into the mountains towards Mgeta Mission station, which is situated about ten miles further into the mountains.

Leaving their horses behind, the men worked their way after the enemy into the mountains, and on the 27th General Nussey, whose brigade had in the meantime joined that Enslin, occupied Mgeta Mission, while Enslin's men, who were moving into the mountains in a more southerly direction with the intention of cutting off the retreat of the enemy, had driven them off Hombossa mountain south-west of Mgeta. At this stage I arrived with General Brits at Mlali and ordered Nussey to follow the enemy through the mountains along the course of the Mgeta River, while Enslin was ordered back to the track which proceeds round the west of the mountains by Mssongossi River and Mahalaka to Kissaki at the southern extremity of the mountains. In this march Enslin's brigade was joined by Beves' two infantry regiments and was accompanied by General Brits.

(43) It was clear to me from the vast quantities of heavy gun ammunition captured at this and various other points in the Uluguru that the enemy had intended a long and elaborate defence of these mountains, and that it was the unexpected arrival of General Enslin at Mlali and the audacious and successful pursuit into the mountains, combined with the operations of General Hoskins' Division on the other side of the mountains, that had forced the enemy to abandon his plans and retreat towards Kissaki. Nussey, followed only by porter transport, slowly worked his way southward through the mountains, finding much ammunition abandoned everywhere.

General Brits, on arriving at Mssongossi River, found that it was impossible to take his guns or wagons any further, and from there they had to return to Morogoro and rejoin him later at Kissaki by the eastern route. From Mahalaka to Kissaki he followed the elephant track which had been the route of Burton and Speke's journey into the interior in 1857. On the 5th September the neighbourhood of Kissaki was reached without any serious opposition. Nussey had not yet arrived and, owing to the roughness of the mountains and some damage to his wireless, no communication could be established with him.

In spite of this, however, General Brits decided to attack Kissaki on the 7th September. Beves was ordered to follow the footpath southward along the Mgeta into Kissaki, while Enslin, with the mounted men, marched round by the right, so as to attack from the west and south-west. Kissaki was found to be strongly held, the bulk of the enemy being on the right bank of the Mgeta in front of Enslin, while dense bush prevented Beves on the other side of the river from offering any effective assistance to the former. The enemy's superior force therefore found it possible first to threaten Enslin's left flank by moving between him and Beves, and when Enslin weakened his right flank to reinforce his left, the pressure of the enemy again became too strong on his right. He therefore decided to retire at night, having lost nine men killed, twelve wounded and seven captured.

Beves was also ordered to withdraw, and the whole force entrenched below Little Whigu hill, six miles north of Kissaki, and awaited the arrival of Nussey. Nussey, who was in ignorance of these events or the position of General Brits, arrived before Kissaki on the morning of the following day, and an action developed, in which he gallantly held his ground against much superior forces till the evening, when General Brits' messengers reached him with an order to withdraw to Little Whigu. His loss had been twenty-three killed and about the same number wounded. Although this action could be heard from Brits' camp, it was found impossible, owing to the ruggedness of the terrain and the thickness of the bush, to go to his assistance.

If communication between Brits and Nussey could have been maintained there is no doubt a joint attack would have led to the capture of Kissaki, whereas the two isolated efforts led to a double retirement and a regrettable recovery of enemy morale. It was only on the 15th September, when General Hannyngton had already captured Dutumi, eighteen miles further east, that General Enslin, by a flank movement round the north-east of Kissaki to Dakawa and the threat to cut off the enemy's retreat to the Rufiji, compelled him to evacuate Kissaki. The enemy had left behind his hospital full of sick and about seventy-two white Germans, but all supplies had been removed or destroyed.

The enemy had now been driven everywhere from the Uluguru mountains, and taken up a defensive line along the Mgeta River south of Dutumi, and further to the west astride the road from Kissaki to the Rufiji. The attack against him along this line was not pressed, as our men were exhausted and worn out with ceaseless fighting and marching for several weeks through most difficult country on half rations or less, and a thorough rest was imperatively necessary, not only on military but also on medical grounds.

Occupation of Dar-Es-Salaam and of South Coast.

(44) Turning now to the coastal operations, which were conducted simultaneously with these movements in the interior. I have already stated that the navy occupied Bagamoyo on 15th August. At this point General Edwards assembled a force of about 1,800 rifles under Colonel Price for the operations against Dar-es-Salaam. This force was divided into two columns, the smaller one marching south to the

Central Railway at the Ruwu bridge with the object, if possible, of seizing that bridge before its destruction by the enemy, and thereafter swinging round towards Dar-es-Salaam; the other and larger column moving down along the coast towards that port. Neither column met any serious opposition on the march, as the enemy, aware of the overwhelming force moving against Dar-es-Salaam, and determined to avoid capture and also anxious to avoid siege operations against a town containing a large German non-combatant population, had decided not to defend the place, and was everywhere falling back before our advance.

Ruwu railway bridge was found completely destroyed. South-west of Ruwu a small German force was found, which was driven south with considerable loss, and the column then marched east towards Dar-es-Salaam. In the meantime, the coastal column, after occupying Kondutschi and Mssassani Bay, had flung its right wing forward and occupied the Mssimbusi River, which flows round Dar-es-Salaam on the west and north. The navy at the same time appeared before Dar-es-Salaam, and on 3rd September the place surrendered, and was occupied by our forces on 4th September.

The enemy forces had left a few days before. One 6-inch gun had been blown up, while the rest of their artillery was taken south. The railway station and harbour works had been effectively destroyed; the s.s. *Tabora*, *König*, and *Mowe* were found sunk in the harbour beyond any hope of being salved; but the *Feldmarschall* has since been recovered, and at comparatively small expense would again be seaworthy. The floating dock is also being salved.

(45) I considered that the time had now come to occupy effectively the whole of the coast, and accordingly made arrangements with the admiral for convoying forces south and co-operating in the seizure of all important points on the coast south of Dar-es-Salaam. In this way Mikindani (13th September), Ssudi Bay (15th September), Lindi (16th September), Kilwa Kissiwani (7th September), Kilwa Kivinge (commonly called Kilwa) (7th September), and Kiswere were all occupied before the end of September.

At Kilwa a strong column was landed for operations, which I proposed to conduct against the enemy from that quarter. This occupation of the southern coast not only helped to pen the enemy up in the interior, but was intended to prevent any assistance from reaching the enemy from oversea.

RESTORATION OF CENTRAL RAILWAY.

(46) The restoration of Dar-es-Salaam harbour and the preparation of Kilwa as bases for our operations in the interior are both matters of some difficulty, and requiring some time to complete. Both are being pushed forward with the utmost energy.

This is also the place to refer to the restoration of the Central Railway for our supply purposes. While the railway track was largely left undamaged by the enemy, the bridges had been carefully demolished. Between Kilossa and Dar-es-Salaam alone about sixty bridges, some of very considerable dimensions, had been wrecked. To restore these so as to carry heavy locomotives would take many months, during which period all further operations would have to remain at a standstill, and an unbearable strain would be put on our enormously stretched-out transport lines from Moschi railhead and Korogwe on the Tanga railway.

The difficulty had been solved for General Van Deventer by a simple but ingenious device of the South African Pioneers under him. This was to restore the bridges with local material so as to carry a weight of about 6 tons, and to narrow the gauge of our heavy motor lorries so that they could run on railway trolley wheels over the line thus restored. A motor tractor with trailer carries 10 to 15 tons of supplies. In this way General Van Deventer had supplied his division over the railway track for the 120 miles advance from Dodoma to Kilossa, and but for this solution of his transport trouble his advance to the Great Ruaha River at this stage would have been a physical impossibility.

As soon as Morogoro was occupied, the same treatment was applied to that section of the line, with the result that since the 6th October the railway track has been open for motor traffic from Dar-es-Salaam to Dodoma, a distance of almost 300 miles, and our forces have been supplied from Dar-es-Salaam as sea base. By the end of October, the railway will thus be open for motor traffic to Tabora, and the restoration and strengthening of the line for heavy locomotive traffic, for which heavy material has to come up from the coast, can proceed as circumstances permit.

NORTHEY'S ADVANCE.

(47) A word more about the western operations will complete the picture of the military situation in German East Africa by the middle of October. Brigadier-General E. Northey, A.D.C., whose operations

229

have been conducted with remarkable ability and vigour, occupied Lupembe on 19th August and Iringa on 29th August; the latter place would have been occupied much earlier but for my advice to him to slow down while the line of retreat of the enemy's forces from the Central Railway was still uncertain. His Lupembe column is now on the Ruhudje River south-west of Mahenge, while his Iringa column is near the Ulanga River north-west of Mahenge. Ssongea in the south has also been occupied. The importance of his role is becoming more accentuated as the campaign progresses and the enemy forces may intend to retire south.

ADVANCE TO TABORA

In the north-west, as already stated, Sir Charles Crewe's advance troops were at Misungi, south of Mwanza, on 16th July, while one Belgian column was farther west near Biaramulo and Namirembe, and a second Belgian column was at Ujiji on Lake Tanganyika on 5th August. It was arranged between General Tombeur and General Crewe that their columns from Lake Victoria should advance simultaneously to St. Michael and Iwingo respectively on the western and eastern roads southward to Tabora. Difficulties of transport supplies and organisation delayed their advance so that General Crewe only reached Iwingo on 7th August and Colonel Molitor's Belgian column could not be concentrated at St. Michael before the 22nd August. The British column reached Schinjanga on the 30th August.

In the meantime, the Belgian Ujiji column under Colonel Olsen had steadily moved forward towards Tabora, and on 1st and 2nd September fought actions with the enemy to the west and south-west of Tabora. General Tombeur therefore decided to push Colonel Molitor's column southward with all possible speed so as to be able to co-operate with Colonel Olsen. Their combined operations caused the enemy to retreat, and the Belgian forces occupied Tabora on the 19th September, while a week later General Crewe's advanced troops occupied the railway at Igalulu, east of Tabora.

The enemy retired in two columns—one under General Wahle eastward along the railway and then southward to the Itumba Mountains; the other under Wintgens southward *via* Sikonge. At the time of writing this report both columns are approaching the Great Ruaha River north and west respectively of Iringa, and Northey's and Van De venter's patrols are in touch with them. Their object is evidently to form a junction with the main enemy forces further east.

Portuguese Advance

In the extreme south General Gil with a Portuguese force has crossed the Rovuma River and occupied certain strategic points to the north of it.

The net result of all these operations at the moment of writing is that the Germans have been driven south over the Central Railway and are now disposed as follows:—In the north-east, on the Rufiji River and about 30 miles to the north of it; in the west, along or south and east of the Great Ruaha River and Ulanga River. With the exception of the Mahenge plateau, they have lost every healthy or valuable part of their colony. In the east they are cut off from the coast, and in the south the Portuguese Army has appeared north of the Rovuma River.

Behaviour of Troops

(48) It would seem fit and proper to add a few words in recognition of the work done by the officers and men whom I have the honour to command. But in view of the foregoing statement of the main facts eulogy seems unnecessary and misplaced. The plain tale of their achievements bears the most convincing testimony to the spirit, determination, and prodigious efforts of all ranks. Their work has been done under tropical conditions which not only produce bodily weariness and unfitness, but which create mental languor and depression, and finally appal the stoutest hearts. To march day by day, and week by week, through the African jungle or high grass, in which vision is limited to a few yards, in which danger always lurks near but seldom becomes visible, even when experienced, supplies a test to human nature often in the long run beyond the limits of human endurance.

And what is true of the fighting troops applies in one degree or another to all the subsidiary and administrative services. The efforts of all have been beyond praise, the strain on all has been overwhelming. May the end soon crown their labours.

Special Services.

(49) I am particularly indebted to the following for their services during the operations:—

Major-General A. R. Hoskins, C.M.G., D.S.O., who has commanded the 1st Division and has rendered me the greatest services by the ability and loyal manner in which he has carried out my orders.

Major-General J. L. Van Deventer, at the head of the 2nd Division, was throughout these operations in command of a widely detached movement, which he conducted in a manner worthy of the highest praise.

Major-General C. J. Brits, in command of the 3rd Division, has invariably co-operated loyally and ably in carrying out my wishes as intended.

Brigadier-General S. H. Sheppard, D.S.O., has, in addition to his services at the head of his brigade, used his great engineering capabilities to the best advantage on many occasions, thereby enabling our advance to proceed unchecked.

Brigadier-General J. A. Hannyngton has proved his worth as a commander in the Field, having been very largely employed in carrying out independent operations.

Brigadier-General P. S. Beves has sustained his high soldierly record, and the 2nd South African Infantry Brigade under him has borne more than its due share of the labours and hardships of the campaign.

Brigadier-General C. A. L. Berrange, C.M.G., at the head of the 3rd South African Infantry Brigade, has rendered excellent service with the 2nd Division and taken a leading share in all the hard work performed by that Division.

Brigadier-General B. G. L. Enslin, by carrying out two arduous turning movements with his mounted brigade, largely contributed to the rapid clearing of the Nguru and the Uluguru Mountains.

Brigadier-General A. H. M. Nussey, D.S.O., has rendered distinguished service, first as General Van Deventer's Chief Staff Officer, and subsequently in command of the 1st Mounted Brigade, in succession to Brigadier-General Manie Botha.

Brigadier-General the Honourable Sir C. P. Crewe, C.B., K.C.M.G., rendered very useful service, first in organising the transport and supply arrangements for General Tombeur's force from Lake Victoria, and subsequently in commanding our advance to Mwanza and Tabora.

My heartiest thanks are due to Rear-Admiral E. F. B. Charlton, C.B., and all ranks of the Royal Navy for the very able and thorough manner in which they have furthered my plans, not only by occupying points on the coast, sometimes even without military assistance, but by enabling a change of base to be carried out first to Tanga and then to Dar-es-Salaam.

The work of the Air Services has been most creditable. In addition to their reconnaissance work, there is evidence to the effect that both material and moral damage has been done to the enemy by their constant bombing raids.

I have already alluded to the amount of engineering work that has had to be carried out. Both in bridge building and road making the engineers and pioneers with the force have worked very hard, and rendered very valuable service.

The Royal Artillery has invariably made the most of any opportunities that have offered for assisting the advance of the infantry.

The Supply and Transport Services have spared no effort to cope with the enormous distances and the difficulties entailed in campaigning in such a vast and undeveloped country.

The manner and rapidity with which the repairs to the Tanga and Central Railways have been effected reflect great credit on all ranks of the Railway Services, and in this connection I should like especially to bring to notice the service rendered by Lieutenant-Colonel C. W. Wilkinson, of the Railway Sappers and Miners, and Major J. H. Dobson, of the South African Pioneers, in carrying out the temporary repairs to the Central Railway which have enabled the troops in the interior to be supplied from Dar-es-Salaam practically within a month of its occupation.

The work of the Medical Units has been very heavy, and all ranks have done their utmost in their care of sick and wounded and in arranging for their speedy evacuation.

The Ordnance Service is to be congratulated on having so successfully met the very varied calls made on it, which success bears testimony to the excellent organisation of that Service.

Great credit is due to the Signal Service for the really excellent way in which communication has been maintained. The operations have been carried on by three widely separated forces, which have each been again sub-divided into two or more columns, and this has strained the resources of the Service to its furthest limits. It has only been by unremitting efforts that success has been achieved.

My thanks are due to the various Political Officers who have accompanied the columns, and by their work materially assisted the operations by helping to gain the confidence of the natives, which is so important a feature in a campaign of this nature.

The Officers of my Staff have given me every assistance.

I would again especially mention the very great debt which I owe to Brigadier-General J. J. Collyer, C.M.G., my Chief of the General Staff, and to Brigadier-General R. H. Ewart, C.B., CLE., D.S.O., A.D.C., Administrative Staff, for the tireless energy and unfailing tact with which they have carried out their respective duties, thereby relieving me of all detail work and leaving me free to devote myself solely to the prosecution of the campaign.

Brigadier-General W. F. S. Edwards, D.S.O., has continued to render valuable services as Inspector-General of Communications, and has from time to time had control of minor operations on lines of communication, which he has always handled to my entire satisfaction.

(50) A dispatch giving the names of the officers and men whose services I also desire to bring to your notice is in course of preparation, and will follow at a later date.

I have the honour to be,
    Sir,
        Your obedient Servant,
            J. C. Smuts, Lieutenant-General,
                Commander-in-Chief,
                East African Force.

9 781782 827092